A Ba
of Invertebrate
Zoology

Ron Clouse

2016

COUNSELOR

B O O K S   L L C

Cover design and painting by Ron Clouse

Author photo by Colin Murphy

Illustrations from *A Manual of Zoology*, Second Edition, 1871, by Henry Alleyne Nicholson

Counselor Books, L.L.C.
counselorbooks.com
counselorbooks@gmail.com

ISBN-13: 978-1530670024
ISBN-10: 1530670020

Contents

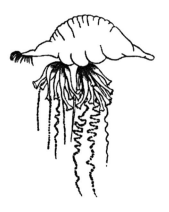

Introduction

This glossary contains over 900 terms commonly encountered in a survey course on invertebrate zoology. Most relate to morphology and development, since body parts and life stages constitute a large set of discrete forms which require a specialized vocabulary to be discussed efficiently. I originally wrote this work when I was a student and laboratory instructor, since at that time there was a lack of study materials, the internet did not yet exist, and accessing original scientific works was much more difficult than it is today. I have maintained the basic choice of terms and formatting I chose over 20 years ago, but the definitions and taxonomy have been updated and improved in light of scientific discoveries made since then.

Students of invertebrate zoology must become fluent in its terminology to be successful, but the lexicon of this field has more problems than just being large. First, no biologist can coordinate it far beyond their own specialty, and thus words coined to avoid confusion in one taxon become sources of such while simultaneously studying groups described by several different scientists. Second, the meanings and taxonomic contexts of many terms are moving targets. Continued advances in microscopy, field biology, and phylogenetics lead to the naming of new lineages and anatomical structures, as well as new hypotheses of homology; consequently, even the most diligent instructor can easily deliver outdated information. Third, students have had limited choices of study materials in the field, and finding a guide that matches one's preferences for comprehensiveness and manageability can be difficult.

The obvious strategy for students today is to look up unknown terms on the internet, and indeed, there one can find photos, videos, and original scientific papers on almost every term presented here. However, relying on the internet for specialized, technical knowledge poses a dilemma for the beginner, which is how to distinguish good information from bad when one has no knowledge of the topic whatsoever. This glossary itself provides an example of the pitfalls of relying on the flotsam and jetsam of the internet. In the early 2000s I provided the rough version of it at that time for free online, and despite the fact that only a few copies were downloaded, my definitions found their way—errors and all—into various online glossaries.

Thus, this book is intended to be a companion that beginners can take to lectures, laboratories, and study sessions to help them navigate the maze of terminology which underlies a course in invertebrate zoology. Invertebrate animals are endlessly fascinating for people from many different backgrounds and interests, and the less time one needs to spend figuring out the names of their appendages, larvae, glands, and such, the more time one has to enjoy their amazing morphologies, behavioral strategies, physiologies, and evolutionary histories.

Organization

This glossary is organized and designed with the student in mind. First, it is anticipated that the reader will want to add to, subtract from, or reorganize parts of this text. Various instructors will likely hold different opinions than mine about the importance, pronunciation, and even definitions of some terms. Moreover, invertebrate zoology is replete with words that are minor variations of each other (like "furca" and "furcula," included here), and in some cases the variations are used by different esteemed specialists of the same group (in the previous example, the springtails). Ultimately, the best terminological tweaks to learn are those of one's professor or close circle of experts. Thus, the printed version of this glossary is inexpensive and contains ample space for notes, and the e-book version can be easily annotated.

Second, I include a simple guide to pronunciation. It does not use phonetic symbols and may disappoint a linguist, but it should provide students a quick opportunity to say unfamiliar words fairly accurately.

Third, this glossary has a short section on Latin and Greek plurals and root words. Having some knowledge of these allows students to be more fluent in their use of scientific terms and taxonomy, and it equips them to deduce the meanings of new terms they will encounter in more specialized courses. I have also combined the Latin and Greek endings and roots in the same lists so that students can compare similarly spelled items and notice they derive from different languages. In addition, I have written the root words with only the key elements needed for their recognition, not every possible form they might take in a modern word.

Fourth, because a significant source of confusion for many terms is that they are specific to certain taxonomic groups or have different meanings for different taxa, a taxonomic hierarchy is included in many definitions. In this hierarchy, different levels are written in different formats and connected by dashes to provide some taxonomic direction for further reading. Different members of the same higher level are separated by a comma and dash, and completely different hierarchies by a comma only. Taxonomic names in the e-book version will break across lines also with a dash, which can look confusing at first, but the whole name can still be selected with one touch.

Fifth, the definitions here are cross-referenced. Some definitions simply refer readers to more commonly used or more inclusive terms, and all synonyms (and near-synonyms, for there are shades of meaning) are summarized at the end. Defined terms used in definitions are italicized, and in cases where reading the definition of an additional word would be clarifying, it is noted with the phrase "See also …" Of course, some italicized words in definitions differ in form from how they are listed, as demanded by their use in the sentence (such as "embryonic" *vs.* "embryo"), but these should not be too difficult to figure out, and in e-books just the root letters can be highlighted for one-touch searching.

Finally, this glossary is brief and meant to simply provide a toehold in invertebrate zoology. No attempt is made to include every term found in the scientific literature, nor all their uses and forms, as such attempts overwhelm beginners and inevitably miss cases (some of which are best forgotten, granted). In addition, structures commonly found in nature and discussed by experts in the plural, such as certain paired appendages or repeated organs, are listed here in the plural. Students in more specialized courses, like entomology, will require additional glossaries, although this one may serve as a good review.

Pronunciation

Most terms are followed by a phonetic guide, which is my best approximation as an American trained in zoology on the East Coast. It is written intuitively, without linguistic symbols, and using my estimation of where syllables break (indicated by dashes) and which ones should be stressed (bolded). There are no pronunciation guides written for common English words, but they are provided for several words one should know from a basic biology course, just as a reminder. The most difficult phonetic aspects to communicate to readers are the vowel sounds, which are listed below, and one should also pay attention to the representations of "c" and "g."

A		E		I	
cape	/kayp/	delete	/dee-**leet**/	ice	/iys/
act	/akt/	heat	/heet/	igloo	/**ig**-loo/
tuna	/**too**-nah/	bet	/bet/		
		gem	/jem/		

O		U		AI, AU, OI, OU	
spoke	/spok/	blue	/bloo/	pair	/peyr/
boat	/bot/	use	/yooz/	auto	/**aw**-to/
auto	/**aw**-to/	spur	/spur/	boil	/boyl/
ox	/ahks/	gut	/guht/	shout	/showt/
igloo	/**ig**-loo/				
dog	/dawg/				

Latin and Greek Singular and Plural Endings

Many foreign words in English are just given English (anglicized) endings, such as "campuses" for the plural of "campus" (instead of "campi"), but this is not usually the case for scientific terms. They were often invented in the process of writing formal scientific descriptions of new taxa, which was historically done in Latin, and they are often not used widely enough to evolve anglicized endings. Nevertheless, although an anglicized plural ending might be wrong, it is at least consistent with the rest of the text, unlike a plural formed using a third language. So, if one does not know the language of origin of a word, one should pluralize it like any other English word.

This rule of thumb is conveniently illustrated by an invertebrate, actually: the octopus. Being of Greek origin, the plural of "octopus" is not the Latin form "octopi," but rather the Greek word "octopodes." However, since this is the well-known name of a much-loved animal, and "octopodes" is a rare plural form that never gained any traction in common parlance, the preferred plural is the anglicized one, octopuses.

The rules governing Latin and Greek plural endings are complex. Latin nouns have three genders (male, female, and neuter), each noun is a member of one of five categories (called "declensions"), and then a noun can be used in one of six cases. Depending on the gender, category, and case, nouns usually have different endings, and they usually change those endings differently to make plurals, emphasis here on "usually." Ancient Greek did not have so many declensions, but it retained dual endings, distinct from singular and plural, which Latin had lost. In addition, although scientific writing is less prone to this than other genres, foreign root words often enter English via other languages (such as Greek via Latin, Latin via French, and Arabic via Old and Middle English), and modifications easily happen *en route*.

The endings below are written in the form "singular : plural," followed by the origin ("L" for Latin, "G" for Greek). Pronunciation, as needed, is between slashes.

a : **ae**   G   chaeta /**kee**-tah/ : chaetae /**kee**-tee/

a : **ae**   L   pupa /**pyoo**-pah/ : pupae /**pyoo**-pee/

ax : **aces**   L   thorax : thoraces /**thor**-ah-seez/

en : **ena**   L   nomen : nomena

ex : **ices**   L   apex : apices /**ay**-pi-seez/

ies : **ies**   L   series : series

is : **es**	L	testis /**tes**-tis/ : testes /**tes**-teez/
is : **ides**	G	aphis /**ay**-fis/ : aphides /**ay**-fi-deez/
ix : **ices**	L	matrix /**may**-triks/: matrices /**may**-tri-seez/
ma : **mata**	G	lemma : lemmata
nx : **nges**	G	pharynx /**feyr**-inks/ : pharynges /fuh-**rin**-jeez/
o : **ones**, **ines**	L	imago /i-**may**-go/ : imagines /i-**may**-guh-neez/
on : **a**	G	phenomenon : phenomena
sis : **ses**	G	analysis : analyses /ah-**nal**-i-seez/
um : **a**	L	phylum : phyla
us : **era**	L	genus : genera
us : **i**	L	cirrus /**seer**-ruhs/ : cirri /**seer**-ree/
us : **us**	L	apparatus : apparatus

Latin and Greek Root Words

The root words below are just a small sample of those encountered across all of biology, but learning them can take the mystery out of hundreds of terms here. Many of them have multiple forms that result from whether they are used as prefixes or suffixes, or whether they have been slightly anglicized. For example, "troph," Greek for "nutrition" or "food," can appear as "trophic," "trophy," "tropho," "trophous," and other forms, depending on the word. I have noted some of these variants when their spelling or pronunciation is potentially confusing, especially in light of other root words.

a	G	without, lacking (as a prefix) **a**coelomate ("lacking a coelom")
acanth	G	spine, thorn **Acantho**cephala ("thorny head")
amphi	G	both kinds, ends or sides, around **Amphi**oxus ("pointed at both ends")
anth	G	flower **Antho**zoa ("flower animals")
annulus	L	small ring (diminutive of *anus*, ring) **Annel**ida ("in the form of little rings")
arch	G	ultimate beginning (from *archein*, begin, rule) **arch**enteron ("starting gut")
arthro	G	joint **Arthro**poda ("joined foot")
asco	G	sac-like (from *askos*, bag, especially wineskin) **asco**noid ("resembling a bag")
aster	G	star **Aster**oidea ("resembling a star")
blast	G	germ, sprout, growth **blast**ula ("little sprout")
brach	G	arm **Brachio**poda ("arm foot")
branch	G	gill **Branchio**poda ("gill foot")
bryo	G	moss **Bryo**zoa ("moss animals")
cephal	G	head **Cephalo**poda ("head foot")
chaeta /**kee**-tah/	G	spine, bristle, long hair **Chaeto**gnatha ("bristle jaw")

chela /**kee**-lah/	G	claw **cheli**ped ("claw foot")
coel /seel/	G	hollow, cavity spongo**coel** ("sponge cavity")
collo /**kah**-lo/	G	glue **collo**blast ("glue cell")
cord, **chord**	G	cord **Chord**ata ("having a cord")
corona	G via L	crown (from *koronos*, something curved) **corona**te larva ("crown-shaped larva")
cnid /nid/	G	nettle (a plant with stinging hairs) **Cnid**aria ("nettle [+ -aria for a taxon]")
crusta	L	shell **Crusta**cea ("shelled")
ctene /teen/	G	comb **Cteno**phora ("bearing combs")
cycl /sikl/	G	wheel, round, circle **Cyclio**phora ("bearing a wheel")
cyst /sist/	G	bladder, pouch nemato**cyst** ("thread pouch")
cyte /siyt/	G	cell (from *kytos*, hollow vessel) cnido**cyte** ("nettle-like [stinging] cell")
cy, **cyo**, **kyo**	G	embryo Di**cy**emida ("two origins [two larvae]")
derm	G	skin meso**derm** ("middle skin")
deutero, **deuter**, **deuto**	G	second or secondary **deutero**stome ("secondary mouth")
di, **dich**	G	two **di**oecious ("two houses [two sexes]")

dino   G   1. whirlpool or eddy (from *dinos*)
                     dinoflagellate ("whirling whip")

                  2. terrible, frightening (from *deinos*)
                     dinosaur ("terrible lizard")

duo, du   L   two
                     duplicate

echin   G   spiny
                     Echinodermata ("having spiny skin")

eco, oec, ec G   house
                     ooe**ec**ium ("egg house")

ecto   G   outside
                     Ectoprocta ("outside anus")

ento   G   inside, within
                     Entognatha ("inside mouth")

entero   G   intestines
                     enterocoely ("intestine cavity")

entomo   G   segmented, cut up, insects
                     entomology ("the study of insects")

epi   G   on, upon, over
                     epicuticle ("on the cuticle")

fer   L   produce, have, bear (See also **phor**.)
                     Pori**fera** ("bearing pores")

fil   L   thread-like
                     filopodium ("thread foot")

gastr   G   Stomach
                     Gastrotricha ("hairy stomach")

gen   G via origin, birth, kind, creation
                  L   **gen**us ("type")

glyph   G   vertical groove (from *glyphe*, carve)
/glif/   siphono**glyph** ("tube groove")

gnath /nath/	G	jaw **Gnatho**stomulida ("jawed, little mouth")
grad, **gree**, **gress**	L	walking, step, moving Palpi**gradi** ("feeler walking")
gymno, **gymn** /**jim**-no/	G	naked **Gymno**laemata ("naked throat")
gyn /giyn or jiyn/	G	female proto**gyn**ous ("first female")
helminth	G	worm Platy**helminth**es ("flat worms")
hemo, hema, **hem**	G	blood **hemo**coel ("blood cavity")
hemi	G	half **Hemi**chordata ("having half of a cord")
holo	G	whole, entire **Holo**thuroidea ("entirely resembling an oblong shield or door")
hydro	G	water **Hydro**zoa ("water animals")
insectum	L	segmented (See also **entomo**.) **insect**
iso	G	equal, identical, similar **Iso**ptera ("similar wings")
kera, cera	G	horn cheli**cera** ("claw horn")
kin	G	move **Kino**rhyncha ("moving snout")
krinon	G	lily **Crin**oidea ("resembling a lily")

labio   L lip
                   labial palps ("lip feelers")

lith   G stone
                   gastro**lith** ("stomach stone")

lob   G via L rounded projection, lobe
                   Tri**lob**ita ("three lobes")

lorica   L corset

malac   G soft (See also **moll**.)
                   malacology (the study of Mollusca)

mastix   G via L whip (Greek *mastig*)
                   *Lepto***mastix** ("delicate whip")

medi   L middle (sometimes altered as "mer")
                   inter**medi**ate ("between, in the middle")

mere   G part, segment (See also **medi**.)
                   meta**mere** ("between segment")

meso, mes   G middle, intermediate
                   mesoglea ("middle glue")

meta, met   G after, behind, between, beyond, changed
                   metamorphosis ("change form")

moll   L soft
                   Mollusca

mon, mono   G one, single
                   Monoplacophora ("bearing one shell")

morph   G shape, appearance
                   Nemato**morpha** ("thread-shaped")

myo, my   G muscle (from *myos* or *mus*, mouse)
                   myocyte ("muscle cell")

Naiad   G From Greek mythology, a naiad was a
                   type of **nymph** (lower-ranked, female,
                   nature deity) associated with lakes,
                   spring, rivers, and ponds (fresh water).

nect, **nek**	G	Swimming Ortho**nect**ida ("straight swimmer")
nemato	G	thread-like **Nemat**oda
nephr	G	kidney **nephr**idium ("little kidney")
Nemertes	G	From Greek mythology, Nemertes was the most insightful and wisest of the **Nereids**; source of the phylum name "Nemertea" and genus name "*Nemertes*."
Nereid	G	A **nymph** (lower-ranked, female, nature deity) associated with the ocean and seas (salt water).
noto	G	back **noto**chord ("back cord")
nymph	G	From Greek mythology, a nymph was a lesser goddess associated with specific features of the landscape (like a river or hill).
oo /o-o/	G	egg, ovum (from *oion*, egg) **oo**zoid ("egg animal")
odont	G	tooth Heter**odonta** ("different teeth")
onkos	G	mass or growth **onco**sphere ("spherical growth")
onych /**aw**-nik/	G	claw **Onycho**phora ("bearing claws")
ophis /o-fis/	G	snake **Ophi**uroidea ("in the form of a snake tail")
ortho	G	straight, correct, true **Ortho**ptera ("straight-winged")

os, or, **ora**	L	mouth ("Os" and "oris" are different forms of the same Latin word.) **os**culum ("little mouth") ab**oral** ("away from the mouth")
os, oss, **ost**	G via L	bone **oss**icle ("little bone")
oxi, oxy	G	sharp, pointed, acidic, pungent **oxy**gen ("acid-making" [archaic science])
palp	L	feel, touch lightly pedi**palp** ("foot feeler")
par, para	G	alongside, among, beside, strange, wrong **para**phyletic ("beside group")
parthenos	G	maiden, virgin **partheno**genesis ("virgin birth")
ped	L	foot Cirri**ped**ia ("tentacle foot")
peri	G	around, surrounding, enclosing, near **peri**cardium ("around the heart")
phag /fayj or fayg/	G	eating eso**phag**us ("carrier of what's eaten")
phor	G via L	produce, have, bear (See also **fer.**) Pogono**phora** ("having a beard")
Phoronis /for-**on**-is/	G	Alternative name for the Greek nymph Io; source of the phylum name "Phoronida" and genus name "*Phoronis*." (See also **nymph**.)
pinn	L	wing or feather bi**pinn**aria ("two wings")
plac, plak, **plat, plax**	G	flat, plate **Platy**helminthes ("flat worms")
plac	L	peace, calm, peaceful **plac**ate

plan	L	flat
		planula ("little flat one")
pneum	G	lung (from *pneuma*, wind, breath, spirit)
		pneumatophore ("bearing a lung")
pod, pode	G	foot
		pseudo**pod** ("false foot")
poly	G	many
		Polyplacophora ("bearing many plates")
por	L via G	pore
		porocyte ("pore cell")
Priapus	G	Minor Greek fertility god associated with agriculture and renowned for his large endowment.
		Priapulida ("shaped like a little penis")
proct	G	anus
		Ento**procta** ("inside anus")
proto, prot	G	first
		protonephridium ("first nephridium" [archaic science])
pseudo, pseud /**soo**-do/	G	false
		pseudochitin ("false chitin")
pter /ter/	G	wing
		Di**ptera** ("two wings")
ptych /tik/	G	a fold
		ptychocyst ("fold pouch")
pus	G	foot
		*Sticho**pus*** ("row foot")
ram	L	branch
		bi**ram**ous ("two branches")

ren	L	kidney
		renette cells ("little kidney cells" [French diminutive])
rhizo, rhiz	G	root
		rhizopodium ("root foot")
rhin, rhynch	G	nose, snout
		rhynchocoel ("snout cavity")
rot, roti	L	wheel
		Rotifera ("bearing a wheel")
sarc /sahrk/	G	flesh
		peri**sarc** ("enclosing the flesh")
schiz /shiz or skiz/	G	division, split
		schizont ("the one that divides")
scolec	G	worm or grub
		scolex
scyph /siyf/	G	cup
		Scyphozoa ("cup animal")
siphon	G	tube
		Sipuncula ("little tube," diminutive)
sit	G	food, eating
		para**site** ("alongside eating")
sphongos	G	sponge (perhaps also the origin of "fungus")
sporo, spor	G	spore
stato	G	standing, used in the sense of:
		1. having a fixed position
		statocyst ("fixed pouch")
		2. surviving
		statoblast ("surviving growth")
stoma	G	mouth, orifice
		hypo**stome** ("below the mouth")

tard	L	slow
		Tardigrada ("slow walking")
theca	G	case, covering
		sperma**theca** ("sperm covering")
thorax	G	breastplate
trich	G	hair
/trik/		**Tricho**plax ("hairy, flat")
troph	G	nutrition, food
/trof/		**tropho**zoite ("food animal")
trop	G	bend, turn, turning
		helio**trop**ism ("sun turning" [growing toward the sun])
troche	G	circular (from *trochos*, wheel)
/trok/		**trocho**phore ("bearing a wheel")
uni, un	L	one, single
		uniramous ("single-branched")
ur, uro	G	1. tail (from *oura*)
		uropod ("tail foot")
		2. urine (from *ouron*)
		uric acid, **ur**ea
xeno	G	different, odd
/**zee**-no/		**Xeno**turbellida ("strange little agitator")
xiphos	G	sword
/**ziy**-fos/		**Xiphos**ura ("sword-tailed")
xyl	G	wood
/ziyl/		**xylo**phagus (eating wood)
zoo, zo, zoa	G	animal
		Cubo**zoa** ("cube animal")

Taxonomy

The aspect of this glossary that has been most revised since its original writing is the taxonomy. The reason for this is simply that in recent years there has been a great proliferation of phylogenetic studies. These have improved not only our understanding of how taxonomic groups at all levels relate, but also our reckoning of homology among similar-looking structures. Thus, many taxonomic names and hierarchies have changed (in some cases retired), as have the taxonomic contexts and appropriate uses of some terms.

Major taxonomic changes have happened in every large group of invertebrates subjected to molecular studies, but not surprisingly they have been most frequent among the single-celled organisms called protists. Their small sizes have allowed them to speciate into a dizzying number of lineages, but this feature also limits their morphological repertoire and our ability to see it. Moreover, their old age contributes to their diversity and has facilitated considerable convergence in their evolution. With DNA sequencing and the profusion of data it provides, we have learned that various protist lineages are more closely related to the big multicellular kingdoms (animals, fungi, and plants) than they are to each other. Nonetheless, for historical and perhaps practical reasons invertebrate zoologists are still expected to master protists as well, at least those which are not too plant-like, such as diatoms and various other non-motile forms.

For protist taxonomy I follow Adl *et. al.* (2005), with the one exception of using "Protista," a name they discard completely. Their taxonomic system is based on "nameless ranked systematics," meaning that although taxonomic groups are organized in a nested, ranked fashion, these ranks do not correspond to traditional categories, such as "Phylum" and "Class." This removes one level of debate from the establishment of nested groups, and it allows their groupings to more quickly adapt as the still-unresolved taxa are clarified. This is why protist names in the taxonomic hierarchies here are written in brackets, the format I use for unranked or informal (but still useful) groups.

For some groups, regardless of what surprises molecular phylogenies held or how homology assessments have been revised, the anatomies and life cycles are just unknown or rarely documented, other than for a few canonical species. This is the case with many jellyfish and their polyp stages, the anatomical and embryological terms for which rely heavily on studies of *Aurelia* and *Obelia*. The degree to which these terms apply to taxa outside of these genera, the scyphozoan subclass Discomedusae, or the class Hydrozoa, is not always clear. I have attempted to highlight such uncertainty by using the word "especially" when referring to groups where I know a term is commonly used but I do not claim it is completely inapplicable to other groups.

In each taxonomic guide associated with a term, names are connected by dashes and ordered from most inclusive to least. Below is the correspondence between taxonomic rank and format. In some cases different ranks have been written in the same format, which was done for simplicity and readability, but their exact position can usually be inferred from their endings and context.

[OBSOLETE OR RANKLESS GROUP]-

KINGDOM-

SUPERPHYLUM-PHYLUM-SUBPHYLUM-

Superclass-**Class**-**Subclass**-**Infraclass**-

Superorder-Order-Suborder-Infraorder-

Family-Subfamily-

Genus-species

A

ABDOMEN /**ab**-do-men/ 1. General term for the region of an organism that contains most of the digestive organs. 2. In crustaceans and hexapods, the part of the body posterior to the *thorax* or *cephalothorax* (ARTHROPODA-CRUSTACEA, -HEXAPODA). 3. Occasional term for the *opisthoma*. 4. In some radiolarian *protists* that make an elongate, *segmented test*, the third and usually largest section (after the *cephalis* and *thorax*, and sometimes followed by *post-abdominal* sections) ([PROTISTA-RHIZARIA-RADIOLARIA-POLYCYSTINA-NASSELLARIA]).

ABORAL /**ab-or**-ahl/ The side of an organism opposite the *mouth* (especially ECHINODERMATA). See also *exumbrella*.

ACETABULUM /a-se-**ta**-byoo-luhm/ 1. The ventral *sucker* of *flukes* that lies posterior to the mouth and oral *sucker* (PLATYHELMINTHES-**Trematoda**). 2. The posterior sucker of leeches (ANNELIDA-**Hirudinea**). 3. Occasionally used to refer to a *sucker* on a cephalopod *arm* (MOLLUSCA-**Cephalopoda**).

ACICULUM /ah-**sik**-yoo-luhm/ The *chitinous* rod supporting the *neuropodium* or *notopodium* (ANNELIDA-**Polychaeta**).

ACOELOMATE /ay-**seel**-lo-mayt/ A type of body plan in which there is solid tissue (*parenchyma*) between the outside of the *alimentary canal* and the inside of the body wall (CYCLIOPHORA, GNATHOSTOMULIDA, PLATYHELMINTHES, [XENACOELOMORPHA]). The list of acoelomate phyla sometimes also includes those poorly studied phyla once referred to as *Mesozoa*, and the developmental stages of two of them (DICYEMIDA, ORTHONECTIDA) are perhaps well studied enough to identify them as acoelomates; however, the placozoans are likely not *triploblastic*, and the monoblastozoans may not even exist. Discussions of *coelom* development pertain only to *triploblastic* phyla, and thus *diploblastic* phyla (Cnidaria and Ctenophora) have not been considered acoelomate, despite lacking a *coelom*. (However, their *mesoglea* does contain certain cells that are suggestive of *mesoderm*, which would change things.) *Sponges* are sometimes considered *diploblastic*, but they may not even undergo true *gastrulation*, and whether they have *germ layers* at all is debatable. See also *coelom* and *pseudocoelomate*.

ACOELOMORPHS /ay-**see**-lo-morfs/ Proposed subphylum of Xenacoelomorpha, containing two groups of simplified marine *animals* that have been historically difficult to place *taxonomically*: Acoela and Nemertodermatida. See also *xenoturbellids* ([XENACOELOMORPHA-ACOELOMORPHA]).

ACONTIUM /ah-**kon**-shyuhm/ The extension of the middle ridge of a *mesenteric filament* at the base of *sea anemones*; it is covered with *nematocysts* and can be extended out through the *mouth* or pores in the body wall (CNIDARIA-**Anthozoa**).

ACORN WORMS Common name for hemichordates (HEMICHORDATA).

ACTINOPHARYNX /**ak**-tin-o-**feyr**-inks/ The tubular extension past the *mouth* and into the *gastrovascular cavity* of *sea anemones* which, although similar to a true *pharynx* in position and function, is derived entirely from the *ectoderm* (CNIDARIA-**Anthozoa** except -**Hexacorallia-**Antipatharia-*Sibopathes*).

ACTINOPODIUM /**ak**-tin-o-**po**-dee-uhm/ See *axopodium*.

ACTINULA /ak-**tin**-yoo-lah/ A *larval polyp* that has a *mouth* and *tentacles* but either drifts in the *plankton* or swims using *cilia* (CNIDARIA-**Hydrozoa**, -**Anthozoa**).

ADDUCTOR MUSCLES /ahd-**duhk**-tor …/ The pair of muscles used by *clams*, mussels, oysters, and other bivalve mollusks to hold their *shells* closed (MOLLUSCA-**Bivalvia**).

ADHESIVE GLAND In rotifers, the *gland* in the *foot* that opens through the *toes* by which the *animal* attaches to the substrate (ROTIFERA). See also *adhesive papillae*.

ADHESIVE PAPILLAE /… pah-**pil**-lee/ The set of *glands* at the anterior end of a tunicate *larva* (*tadpole larva*) used in attaching to the substrate (CHORDATA-TUNICATA).

ADRADIAL CANALS /ad-**ray**-dee-uhl …/ In scyphozoan *medusae*, those *radial canals* that lead directly from the sides of the *gastric pouches* to the *ring canal* (CNIDARIA-**Scyphozoa**). See also *interradial canals* and *perradial canals*.

ADULT A sexually mature individual. For insects (ARTHROPODA-HEXAPODA-**Insecta**) a special term, *imago*, is sometimes used.

AFFERENT /**af**-fer-ent/ Incoming or approaching, as opposed to *efferent*.

AHERMATYPIC /**ay**-**hur**-mah-**ti**-pik/ A type of *coral* that does not build *reefs* (generally CNIDARIA-**Anthozoa** except -**Hexacorallia**-<u>Scleractinia</u>).

ALECITHAL /ay-**le**-se-thuhl/ A type of *egg* that lacks *yolk*.

ALIMENTARY CANAL /ay-li-**men**-tuh-ree …/ The tube or hollow in which food is processed and nutrients are absorbed; it may have one opening (*incomplete gut*) or two openings (*complete gut*) (not found in [ACANTHOCEPHALA], ANNELIDA-**Polychaeta**-<u>Canalipalpata</u>-Siboglinidae [deep-sea worms that include the former phyla Pogonophora and Vestimentifera], [MESOZOA], and PLATYHELMINTHES-**Cestoda**; vestigial in NEMATOMORPHA]; inapplicable to PORIFERA). Synonymous with "gut."

ALVEOLA /**al**-vee-o-lah/ **pl. alveolae** /**al**-vee-o-lee/ A pit or small depression. See also *alveolus*.

ALVEOLUS /**al**-vee-o-luhs/**pl. alveoli** /**al**-vee-o-lee/ An empty sac or cavity. See also *alveola*.

AMBULACRAL GROOVE /am-byoo-**lak**-ral …/ The elongate indentation on the *oral* side of asteroid *arms*, between the *mouth* and tip, from which the *tube feet* project (ECHINODERMATA-**Asteroidea**).

AMETABOLISM /**ay**-me-**ta**-buh-luhs/ Type of primitive insect development in which the *juveniles* do not undergo drastic morphological changes (other than size) before they become *adults* (ARTHROPODA-HEXAPODA-**Entognatha**, -**Insecta**-**Apterygota**). See also *hemimetabolism* and *holometabolism*.

AMICTIC /ay-**mik**-tik/ In rotifers, describing females that develop from unfertilized *diploid eggs* and the *eggs* they produce (ROTIFERA).

AMOEBOCYTES /uh-**mee**-bo-siyts/ *Amoeboid animal* cells. In *sponges* they constitute most of the living cells of the *mesohyl*, are usually specialized for *spicule* formation and food processing, and are sometimes undifferentiated (*archeocytes*) or are former *choanocytes* or *pinacocytes*.

AMOEBOID /uh-**mee**-boyd/ Describing a state of being highly plastic, blob-like, and crawling via the extension and retraction of different parts of one's shape, like members of the *protist* genus *Amoeba* ([PROTISTA-AMOEBOZOA-TUBULINEA-TUBULINIDA]-*Amoeba*).

AMPHIBLASTULA /am-fi-**blas**-chyoo-lah/ One of two main *larval* types in *sponges* after the *stomoblastula* turns inside out (the other being the *parenchymula*); this change creates an outwardly *flagellated*, hollow ball of cells; some cells that lack *flagella* may be *photoreceptors*; mostly in *calcareous sponges*; the *flagellated* cells later invaginate and are covered by the larger, *unflagellated* cells, and the *flagella* again point toward the interior of the *larva*; it then settles, the invagination closes, and it then becomes an *olynthus* (PORIFERA).

AMPHID /**am**-fid/ The anterior organ in nematodes that may be a *chemoreceptor* (NEMATODA). See also *phasmid* (1).

AMPHIDISK /**am**-fi-disk/ A type of large *spicule* in *sponges* (that is, a *macrosclere*) that aids in building the covering of *gemmules* (PORIFERA-**Demospongiae**- Haplosclerida-Spongillidae).

AMPHIOXUS /am-fee-**ahk**-suhs/ **pl. amphioxi** /am-fee-**ahk**-see/ A common name for a member of the chordate subphylum Cephalochordata, taken from the now obsolete genus name for the well-studied European species, *Branchiostoma lanceolatum* (CHORDATA-CEPHALOCHORDATA). Synonymous with "lancelet."

AMPULLA /**am**-pyoo-lah/ 1. The muscle-lined sac used in extending and contracting *tube feet* (ECHINODERMATA). 2. In *protists*, part of the *osmoregulatory* system that moves water from the *cytoplasm* to the *contractile vacuole* ([PROTISTA]).

AMYLASE /**am**-i-lays/ An enzyme that breaks down carbohydrates.

ANAEROBIC /an-er-o-**bik**/ Molecular processes or organisms that occur in *anoxic* conditions (lacking oxygen).

ANAL PORE 1. Either of the two openings connecting the *aboral stomach pouches* of ctenophores to the outside; although wastes do leave the body through them, and they appear to have *sphincter*-like control, it is commonly believed that neither is a true *anus embryologically* (CTENOPHORA). 2. Any pore (and presumably a *gland* opening) near the *anus*, as is common in several arachnids (ARTHROPODA-CHELICERATA-**Arachnida**).

ANALOGOUS /ah-**nal**-uh-guhs/ Similar in design or function because of convergent evolution. See also *homologous*.

ANCESTRAL Describing a trait that has been inherited from a relatively more distant ancestor.

ANECDYSIS /**an**-ek-**diy**-sis/ Stage of arthropod *molting* during which the *animal* slowly hardens the *exoskeleton* but is neither preparing for nor recovering from *ecdysis*

(ARTHROPODA). Also called "intermolt." See also *ecdysis*, *metecdysis*, and *proecdysis*.

ANIMAL Any member of the Kingdom Animalia, all of which are *eukaryotic*, multicellular, and, in most cases, *heterotrophic* and motile. Synonymous with "metazoan."

ANIMAL POLE The hemisphere of the *blastula* that is comprised of small cells (*micromeres*) which divide more rapidly than those of the *vegetal pole*.

ANNULUS /**an**-yoo-luhs/ 1. In dinoflagellates, referring to the groove containing the transverse *flagellum*, or, less commonly, this groove only if it is spiraled and makes more than one ring around the organism (otherwise called a *girdle*) ([PROTISTA-CHROMALVEOLATA-ALVEOLATA-DINOZOA-DINOFLAGELLATA]). See also *sulcus*. 2. An apparent *segment* that does not actually extend to the internal organs or *coelom* (NEMATODA, ANNELIDA-**Hirudinea**). See also *metamere*.

ANOXIC /an-**ahk**-sik/ Describing environments that lack oxygen. See *anaerobic*.

ANTENNAE /an-**ten**-nee/ **sing. antenna** /an-**ten**-uh/ *Appendages* specialized for *chemoreception* and *mechanoreception*, especially in insects, myriapods, crustaceans, and *velvet worms* (especially ARTHROPODA-CRUSTACEA, -HEXAPODA, -MYRIAPODA, ONYCHOPHORA).

ANTENNAL GLAND /an-**ten**-uhl .../ In crustaceans, the main organ used in *excretion* and *osmoregulation* (ARTHROPODA-CRUSTACEA). Synonymous with "green gland."

ANTRUM /**an**-truhm/ See *bursa*. See also *atrium*, *cecum*, *diverticulum*, *lumen*, and *sinus*.

ANUS The opening through which digestive wastes leave a *complete gut*.

APODEME /**a**-po-deem/ In arthropods, a thickened infolding of the *cuticle* used for muscle attachment (ARTHROPODA).

APOPYLE /**a**-po-piyl/ In *sponges*, the opening through which water leaves a *flagellated chamber* (PORIFERA).

APPENDAGE Any body part, usually elongate and/or functionally specialized, that extends from the main body, *trunk*, or *cephalized* region of an organism.

ARBORESCENT /**ar**-bor-**es**-sent/ Branching and tree-like, commonly used to refer to a type of ectoproct colony (ECTOPROCTA for example *Bugula*). See also *encrusting* and *stoloniferous*.

ARCHENTERON /ark-**en**-ter-on/ The internal tube or cavity of the early *embryo*, usually formed during *gastrulation*; it eventually becomes the animal's *alimentary canal*. See also *blastopore* and *stereogastrula*.

ARCHEOCYTES /**ark**-ee-o-siyts/ In *sponges*, undifferentiated *amoebocytes* (PORIFERA).

ARISTOTLE'S LANTERN The feeding apparatus of *sea urchins* and *sand dollars* (although much flattened in the latter); not found in *heart urchins* (ECHINODERMATA-**Echinoidea**).

ARM 1. An echinoderm *appendage* (ECHINODERMATA). 2. One division of the branched *foot* of a cephalopod (MOLLUSCA-**Cephalopoda**).

ARROW WORMS Common name for chaetognaths (CHAETOGNATHA).

ARTICLE One *segment* of an arthropod *appendage*.

ASCONOID /**as**-kuh-noyd/ The simplest type of *sponge* body plan, in which *flagellated* cells line the *spongocoel* (PORIFERA). See also *leuconoid* and *syconoid.*

ASCOPORE /**as**-ko-por/ In ectoprocts, the opening to the *compensation sac* (also called an "ascus," thus the term) (ECTOPROCTA).

ASCUS /**as**-kuhs/ see *compensation sac.*

ATOLL /**a**-tahl/ A type of island that is formed when the top of an underwater volcano, which was once above water, sinks below the surface, leaving only its attached *coral reef* in a ring around a shallow body of water (the lagoon). The growth of *coral* and other organisms keeps the *reef* near the ocean surface, and the ring grows larger in both thickness and diameter due to the greater availability of nutrients on the outside (ocean side) of the atoll. Terrestrial habitat forms via the colonization of *coral* rubble and sand thrown on top of the *reef* during storms. Eventually the sinking of the underlying island as it cools and moves tectonically away from the volcanically active area overcomes *reef* growth, and the atoll submerges completely.

ATRIAL SIPHON or ATRIAL CANAL /**ay**-tree-uhl …/ In tunicates, the opening that carries water, wastes, and *gametes* from the organism (CHORDATA-TUNICATA). Synonymous with "excurrent siphon/canal" and "exhalant siphon/canal" in tunicates (see both for other taxa).

ATRIOPORE /**ay**-tree-o-**por**/ A small, ventral opening on cephalochordates, which is anterior to the *anus* and is the exit for water that has passed through the *pharynx* and *pharyngeal slits* (CHORDATA-CEPHALOCHORDATA).

ATRIUM /**ay**-tree-uhm/ 1. Generally, any body or organ cavity. See also *antrum, bursa, cecum, diverticulum, lumen,* and *sinus.* 2. Used specifically for the part of a heart that is designed to receive *blood.* 3. See *spongocoel.*

ATTACHMENT DISC In entoprocts, the point at which one or several *stalked* individuals attach to the substrate (ENTOPROCTA).

AURICULARIA /ah-**rik**-yoo-**lar**-ee-ah/ **pl. auriculariae** /ah-**rik**-yoo-**lar**-ee-ee/ In *sea cucumbers,* the *larva* after about three days of development; similar to the *bipinnaria larva* (ECHINODERMATA-**Holothuroidea**).

AUTOTOMY /aw-**taw**-to-mee/ The self-amputation of an *appendage* or other body part, often for defense and triggered by rapid biochemical and physiological changes at the point of attachment (especially ECHINODERMATA). See also *regeneration.*

AUTOTROPHIC /**aw**-to-**tro**-fik/ Being able to produce one's own food, either by photo- or chemosynthesis.

AUTOZOOID /**aw**-to-**zo**-id/ One of two main types of ectoproct *zooid,* the feeding *polyp;* autozooids constitute the majority of a colony (ECTOPROCTA). See also *heterozooid.*

AVICULARIUM /ah-**vik**-yoo-**lar**-i-um/ In gymnolaemate ectoprocts, a highly specialized *heterozooid* that removes debris and organisms from the colony surface (ECTOPROCTA-**Gymnolaemata**). See also *vibraculum.*

AXIAL CELL /**ak**-see-uhl …/ The large reproductive cell that extends down the middle of a dicyemid; it may give rise asexually to a *vermiform larva,* or produce *eggs* and *sperm* that join to produce an *infusoriform larva* (DICYEMIDA).

AXIAL GLAND /**ak**-see-uhl …/ See *axial organ.*

AXIAL LOBE /**ak**-see-uhl …/ In trilobites the middle longitudinal lobe of the body (ARTHROPODA-TRILOBITA).

AXIAL ORGAN /**ak**-see-uhl …/ Organ of *glandular* composition surrounding the *stone canal* in asteroids and echinoids (ECHINODERMATA-**Asteroidea**, -**Echinoidea**). Synonymous with "axial gland."

AXOCOEL /**aks**-o-seel/ In echinoderm *embryos*, the most anterior of the three *coelomic* pouches formed by division of the original outpocketing of the *archenteron* (ECHINODERMATA). See also *hydrocoel* and *somatocoel.*

AXOPODIUM /**aks**-o-**po**-dee-uhm/ A thin *pseudopodium* in certain *protists* composed of a rigid central rod of *microtubules* surrounded by *cytoplasm* ([PROTISTA especially -RHIZARIA]). See also *filopodium.*

AXOSTYLE /**aks**-o-stiyl/ *Protist organelle* composed of *microtubules* extending from the *flagellar* bases (*basal body*) at one end through the cell to the other end ([PROTISTA-EXCAVATA, especially -FORNICATA-EOPHARYNGIA-DIPLOMONADIDA, -FORNICATA-EOPHARYNGIA-RETORTAMONADIDA, -PREAXOSTYLA-OXYMONADIDA, -PARABASALIA]). See also *pelta-axostyle complex.*

B

BARNACLES /**bahr**-nah-kulz/ Members of the crustacean infraclass Cirripedia. As *larvae* these *animals* attach themselves by their heads to the substrate and spend the remainder of their lives as *sessile filter-feeders* with a protective covering (ARTHROPODA-CRUSTACEA-**Maxillopoda-Cirripedia**).

BASAL BODY /**bay**-suhl .../ An *organelle* close to the cell surface from which arises a *flagellum* or *cilia*. Synonymous with "kinetosome."

BASAL DISC /**bay**-suhl .../ In cnidarians, the point of attachment of a *polyp* to the substrate (CNIDARIA).

BASKET STARS Common name for *filter-feeding* ophiuroids with extensively branched *arms* (ECHINODERMATA-**Ophiuroidea**).

BEETLES /**bee**-tulz/ Insects in the order Coleoptera, which are distinguished by their hardened forewings (*elytra*) and unparalleled evolutionary success (approximately 350,000 named species, more than any other group of organisms) (ARTHROPODA-HEXAPODA-**Insecta**-Coleoptera).

BELL The primary, circular, *mesoglea*-thickened body of a cnidarian *medusa*, in the center of which is the *mouth* and the associated *manubrium* or *oral arms*, and around the margin of which are *tentacles*, *rhopalia*, a *velarium*, and/or a *velum* (CNIDARIA).

BENTHOS /**ben**-thos/ Collective term for the plants, *animals*, and other organisms living on or close to the bottom of any body of water, including the shore and tidal pools. The adjective "benthic" describes this zone and anything found in it.

BILATERAL SYMMETRY /biy-**lat**-ur-ahl …/ Body plan in which an organism can theoretically be divided into identical halves by cutting along only one particular plane down its central axis.

BINARY FISSION /**biy**-neyr-ee/ Mode of asexual reproduction in which the complete organism divides to produce two equal daughter organisms; common in *protists* ([PROTISTA]). See also *homothetogenic fission* and *symmetrogenic fission*.

BIOLUMINESCENCE /**biy**-o-loo-mi-**ne**-sens/ Light emitted from biological processes (especially ARTHROPODA-HEXAPODA-**Insecta**, CNIDARIA, CTENOPHORA, [PROTISTA-CHROMALVEOLATA-ALVEOLATA-DINOZOA-DINOFLAGELLATA]-*Noctiluca*).

BIPINNARIA /biy-pin-**nar**-ee-ah/ *Bilaterally symmetrical larva* of asteroids that has two *ciliated* bands used in feeding and locomotion; these bands form several curves over the body and then extend on to the first two arms that form later; the *brachiolaria* stage is next (ECHINODERMATA-**Asteroidea**).

BIRADIAL SYMMETRY /biy-**ray**-dee-uhl …/ Body plan in which an organism can theoretically be divided into equal halves by cutting along either of two different planes through its central axis.

BIRAMOUS /biy-**ray**-muhs/ Describing an *appendage* that has two branches (especially ANNELIDA-**Polychaeta**, ARTHROPODA-CHELICERATA-**Merostomata-**<u>Xiphosura</u>, -CRUSTACEA, -TRILOBITA). Recent studies in developmental biology and molecular *phylogenetics* suggest that biramous and *uniramous appendages* can each be the result of different developmental processes and have evolved independently more than once in the arthropods. See also *endite*, *endopodite*, *epipodite*, *exite*, *exopodite*, and *protopodite*.

BLADDER Any sac or cavity used to store liquids or gases.

BLADDER WORM See *cysticercus*.

BLASTOCOEL /**blas**-to-seel/ The fluid-filled space within a *blastula*; it does not become the *archenteron* but is pushed aside during *gastrulation*. See also *stereoblastula*.

BLASTOMERES /**blas**-to-meerz/ Cells that result from *cleavage*, sometimes differentiated into *macromeres* and *micromeres*.

BLASTOPORE /**blas**-to-por/ The point on the *blastula* where the *archenteron* usually begins forming during *gastrulation*, and which becomes the first opening to the *archenteron*.

BLASTOSTYLE /**blas**-to-stiyl/ The extension of the *coenosarc* (internal tissues) in a reproductive *polyp* of a hydrozoan colony that gives rise to the *medusae* (CNIDARIA-**Hydrozoa**).

BLASTULA /**blas**-chyoo-lah/ The early *embryo* that is a roughly spherical mass of cells, often hollow, and lacking openings or invaginations on its surface. See also *blastocoel*.

BLOOD General term for any fluid that circulates through the body, bringing oxygen, nutrients, and hormones to cells, removing carbon dioxide and *nitrogenous wastes*, and transporting *glandular* outputs. See also *hemolymph*.

BOOK GILLS The six pairs of flat, flexible, and page-like respiratory structures on the ventral *opisthoma* of a *horseshoe crab* (ARTHROPODA-CHELICERATA-**Merostomata**-Xiphosura).

BOOK LUNGS The respiratory structures of some arachnids consisting of a *sclerotized* evagination of the ventral *opisthoma* set within a chamber; the opening to the chamber is narrow and sometimes called a *spiracle*; chambers and openings may be paired, and there can be up to four pairs (ARTHROPODA-CHELICERATA-**Arachnida**-Amblypygi, -Araneae, -Schizomida, -Scorpiones, -Thelyphonida). In other arachnids the book lungs have been extensively modified into a *tracheal* system (for example ARTHROPODA-CHELICERATA-**Arachnida**-Acari, -Opiliones).

BOX JELLYFISH Common name for members of the cnidarian class Cubozoa (CNIDARIA-**Cubozoa**). See also *jellyfish*.

BRACHIAL VALVE /**bray**-kee-uhl …/ See *dorsal valve*.

BRACHIOLARIA /bra-kee-o-**leyr**-ee-uh/ *Bilaterally symmetrical larval* stage of *sea stars* following the *bipinnaria*, which has elongate *arms* and a more concentrated *ciliated* band; this stage attaches to the substrate to *bud* off the young *sea star* (ECHINODERMATA-**Asteroidea**).

BRANCHIAL HEART /**brank**-ee-ahl …/ Pumping organ that sends deoxygenated *blood* to where it can acquire oxygen (ANNELIDA, especially MOLLUSCA-**Cephalopoda**).

BRITTLE STARS Common name for ophiuroids, with the exception of *basket stars* (ECHINODERMATA-**Ophiuroidea**).

BROOD CHAMBER 1. Generally, any enclosure used to rear young through several *embryonic* and even *larval* stages. 2. In some branchiopod crustaceans, the dorsal cavity used to rear young (ARTHROPODA-CRUSTACEA-**Branchiopoda**-**Phyllopoda**-**Diplostraca** for example <u>Cladocera</u>-*Daphnia*). 3. In fairy shrimp, an *egg* sac made from an extension of the *uterine* chamber, sometimes also called a "brood pouch" or "brood sac") (ARTHROPODA-CRUSTACEA-**Branchiopoda**-**Sarsostraca**-<u>Anostraca</u>).

BROWN BODY A degenerated ectoproct *polypide* (mainly the *alimentary canal* and associated tissues) after absorbing *nitrogenous wastes*; it is then either *egested* by the *regenerated gut* or moves to the *coelom*; when the *coelom* is filled with brown bodies, the *zooid* will no longer be able to *regenerate* a new *gut* and will die (ECTOPROCTA).

BRYOZOA /**briy**-uh-**zo**-ah/ Former and still commonly used name for the phylum Ectoprocta, used even earlier for the combination of Ectoprocta and Entoprocta.

BUCCAL /**buhk**-ulıl/ Relating to the mouth. Synonymous with "oral."

BUCCAL BULB /**buhk**-uhl …/ In *chitons*, the mass of muscle and other tissue that supports and operates the *radula* and *mouth* (MOLLUSCA-**Polyplacophora**).

BUCCAL CAVITY /**buhk**-uhl …/ A hollow space that follows a *mouth*; also called an "oral cavity."

BUCCAL CIRRI /**buhk**-uhl **seer**-ree/ *Tentacles* around the *mouth* of a cephalochordate (CHORDATA-CEPHALOCHORDATA).

BUCCAL DIVERTICULUM /**buhk**-uhl …/ In *acorn worms*, the anterior extension of the *buccal cavity* (HEMICHORDATA).

BUCCAL SIPHON or BUCCAL CANAL /**buhk**-uhl …/ The opening through which water enters into the *pharyngeal basket* of tunicates (CHORDATA-TUNICATA). Synonymous with "incurrent siphon/canal," "inhalant siphon/canal," and "oral siphon/canal" in tunicates (see *incurrent siphon/canal* and *inhalant siphon/canal* for other taxa).

BUDDING A form of asexual reproduction in which a new individual begins as a growth (a "bud") on the parent and eventually detaches to function independently.

BUGS As a broad, informal term, this is often used to refer to any insects or even any small, terrestrial arthropods; however, it is actually the accepted common name for hemipteran insects, especially those in the suborder Heteroptera (ARTHROPODA-HEXAPODA-**Insecta**-Hemiptera especially -Heteroptera).

BURSA /**bur**-sa/ **pl. bursae** /**bur**-see/ Any sac or pouch. Synonymous with "antrum." See also *genital bursa* and *seminal bursa*, as well as *atrium, cecum, diverticulum, lumen,* and *sinus.*

BURSA COPULATRIX /**bur**-sa **kahp**-yoo-**lay**-triks/ *Gland* present in many land *snails* that is "gametolytic" (breaks down *gametes*) and used by *sperm* recipients to avoid fertilization; these *animals* are simultaneous *hermaphrodites* (have male and female reproductive systems at the same time), but the best reproductive strategy for individuals is usually to be the *sperm* donor and not the recipient

(MOLLUSCA-**Gastropoda**-[PULMONATA]). See also *love dart* and *hypodermic impregnation*.

BYSSUS /**bis**-sus/ In *sessile* bivalve *adults* and many *larval* bivalves, the structure used to attach the organism to the substrate; it consists of "byssal threads," composed of keratin and other proteins, secreted by a *gland* located at the posterior end of the *foot* (MOLLUSCA-**Bivalvia**).

C

CAECUM /**see**-kuhm/ See *cecum*.

CALCAREOUS /kal-**keyr**-ee-uhs/ made from calcium carbonate.

CALCIOBLAST /**kal**-see-o-blast/ A type of *spicule*-forming cell (*scleroblast*) in *sponges* that makes *spicules* out of calcium carbonate (PORIFERA). See also *silicoblast*.

CALYMMA /kah-**lim**-mah/ The *cytoplasm* of radiolarians that lies outside the *central capsule* membrane and gives rise to the *axopodia* ([PROTISTA-RHIZARIA-RADIOLARIA]). See also *endoplasm* and *heliozoa*.

CALYX /**kay**-liks/ 1. The *aboral* body wall of crinoids, which surrounds the bases of the *tentacles* and out of which grows the *stalk* (ECHINODERMATA-**Crinoidea**). 2. The part of an entoproct that holds the digestive organs and the *tentacles* (ENTOPROCTA).

CAPITATE TENTACLES /**kap**-i-tayt …/ In hydrozoan *polyps*, those *tentacles* that are club-shaped, with *cnidocytes* concentrated on the knob ends, and usually found around the *mouth* (CNIDARIA-**Hydrozoa**). See also *filiform tentacles*.

CAPITULUM /kah-**pi**-tyoo-luhm/ In *barnacles*, the part of the organism enclosed in a hard covering and holding most of the organs (essentially all of the animal except for the *peduncle*) (ARTHROPODA-CRUSTACEA-**Maxillopoda-Cirripedia**).

CARAPACE /**keyr**-ah-pays/ Any single, hardened shield that covers the dorsal part of an *animal*; common in arthropods as the plate of *exoskeleton* that covers the *cephalothorax*, *cephalon*, or *thorax* (especially ARTHROPODA).

CARDIAC STOMACH 1. In asteroids and ophiuroids, the more *oral* of two main cavities in the *alimentary canal*; this *stomach* can be everted out of the mouth (ECHINODERMATA-**Asteroidea**, -**Ophiuroidea**). 2. The *stomach* in crustaceans that is nearer to the *mouth* (ARTHROPODA-CRUSTACEA). See also *pyloric stomach*.

CARRIER CELL *Sponge choanocyte* that has lost its *flagellum* and *collar* and is now in the *mesohyl*, carrying the *spermiocyst* and moving toward the *ovum* (PORIFERA).

CATERPILLAR /**kat**-ah-**pil**-ahr/ The *larva* of a moth, skipper, butterfly, or other lepidopteran insect; it has both *thoracic legs* and *prolegs* (ARTHROPODA-HEXAPODA-**Insecta**-Lepidoptera).

CAUDAL /**kaw**-dahl/ Posterior or tail-like.

CECUM /**see**-kuhm/ Any outpocketing of an anatomical tract (reproductive, digestive, etc.); alternative spelling "caecum." See also *diverticulum*, as well as *antrum*, *atrium*, *bursa*, *lumen*, and *sinus*.

CENTRAL CAPSULE In radiolarians, the inner region of the cell, containing the *endoplasm*, and within that the nucleus and other *organelles*; the central capsule is defined by a perforated, often pigmented membrane made of *chitin* or *tectin*; this membrane is not the same as the complex *test*, which is made of silica ([PROTISTA-RHIZARIA-RADIOLARIA]). See also *calymma* and *heliozoa*.

CENTROLECITHAL /**sen**-tro-**les**-i-thahl/ Type of *egg* that has its *yolk* in the very center of the *cytoplasm*, such that the initial *meroblastic cleavage* of the *zygote* happens all around the *embryo*.

CEPHALIS /se-**fa**-lis/ The small capsule at one end of certain radiolarian *tests* ([PROTISTA-RHIZARIA-RADIOLARIA-POLYCYSTINA-NASSELLARIA]). See also *abdomen* (4).

CEPHALIZATION /**se**-fah-li-**zay**-shuhn/ The process by which sense and often feeding organs evolve such that they are concentrated at one end of the body, creating a head.

CEPHALON /**se**-fah-lawn/ The anterior section of trilobites bearing the *eyes*, *mouth*, and *antennae*; composed of five or more fused *segments*; it was covered by a *carapace*, which usually had a flange or extension on the ventral side (ARTHROPODA-TRILOBITA).

CEPHALOTHORAX /se-fah-lah-**thor**-aks/ The body region resulting from the fusion of the head and *thorax* (ARTHROPODA especially -CRUSTACEA).

CERATA /suh-**rah**-tah/ Evaginations of the body wall of some nudibranchs (marine, *shell*-less, often colorful mollusks) that contain outpocketings of the *alimentary canal* (MOLLUSCA-**Gastropoda**-[NUDIBRANCHIA]). See also *cnidosacs*.

CERCARIA /ser-**kar**-ee-ah/ In *digenetic flukes*, the *larval* stage following the *redia* and preceding the *metacercaria*; it usually enters the second *intermediate host*, where it *encysts* (PLATYHELMINTHES-**Trematoda**).

CERCI /**ser**-see/ Paired, jointed, *abdominal appendages* used in *mechanoreception*, *chemoreception*, pinching, or *silk*-making (symphylans); found on the 11th *abdominal segment* of many insects and the 13th *segment* of symphylans (ARTHROPODA-HEXAPODA especially -**Insecta**, MYRIAPODA-**Symphyla**).

CHAETA or CHETA /**kee**-tah/ **pl. chaetae or chetae** /**kee**-tee/ See *seta*.

CHAGGA'S DISEASE /**chah**-gahz …/ Common name for the affliction that is caused by *Trypanosoma cruzi* ([PROTISTA-EXCAVATA-EUGLENOZOA-KINETOPLASTEA-METAKINETOPLASTINA]-*Trypanosoma*) and spread by "kissing *bugs*" (ARTHROPODA-HEXAPODA-**Insecta**-Hemiptera).

CHELA /**kee**-lah/ **adj. chelate** /**kee**-layt/ The grasping termination of an arthropod *appendage* (i.e., a claw) formed by the final *article* being able to press against a long extension of the penultimate *article* (ARTHROPODA-CHELICERATA, -CRUSTACEA). See also *subchelate*.

CHELICERAE /kee-**lis**-uhr-ee/ **sing. chelicera** /kee-**lis**-uhr-ah/ The first pair of *appendages* in the arthropod subphylum Chelicerata; they are used in feeding and are often highly modified in arachnids (ARTHROPODA-CHELICERATA). Sometimes written as "chelicers" (sing. "chelicer").

CHELIPED /**kee**-li-ped/ An *appendage* that terminates in a *chela*, especially the fourth *thoracic appendage* of decapods (*crabs*, lobsters, and their allies) (ARTHROPODA-CHELICERATA, -CRUSTACEA especially -**Malacostraca**-Decapoda).

CHEMOSENSORY, CHEMORECEPTOR, and CHEMORECEPTION The ability to detect, organ for detecting, and act of detecting chemicals (respectively).

CHITIN /**kiy**-tin/ A strong yet flexible carbohydrate found in arthropod *exoskeletons*, as well as in certain hard mouthparts and internal structures of mollusks (e.g., the *radula* and *gladius*) (for example ARTHROPODA, MOLLUSCA). It is stronger than cellulose, the carbohydrate that composes plant cell walls, although it is similar in molecular structure. Fungal cell walls are also made of chitin. See also *tectin*.

CHLORAGOGEN TISSUE /klor-ah-**go**-gen …/ Tissue composed of yellowish cells that surrounds the *intestine* in most annelids and performs many of the functions found in vertebrate livers, such as protein deamination, synthesis of glycogen (a glucose polymer used for energy storage), and hemoglobin production (ANNELIDA).

CHOANOCYTE /ko-**an**-o-siyt/ Type of cell with a collar of *microvilli* surrounding one *flagellum*; it is the main food-gathering cell of *sponges* ([PROTISTA-OPISTHOKONTA-CHOANOMONADA], PORIFERA). Synonymous with "collar cell."

CHOANODERM /ko-**an**-o-derm/ A layer of cells in *sponges* that is composed of *choanocytes* and lines the internal chambers of the *animal* (PORIFERA).

CHROMATOPHORES /kro-**mat**-uh-fors/ Any cells that have the ability to change their pigment content or presentation. In cephalopods, these cells are controlled by the nervous system and hormones, and they expand or contract to expose their pigment. In crustaceans, the cells are fixed in size but can change the number of

pigment granules present at any time (MOLLUSCA-
Cephalopoda, ARTHROPODA-CRUSTACEA,
ECHINODERMATA-**Echinoidea**).

CHRYSALIS /**kris**-ah-lis/ The *pupal* stage of butterflies
(ARTHROPODA-HEXAPODA-**Insecta**-Lepidoptera).

CILIA /**sil**-ee-ah/ **sing. cilium** /**sil**-ee-uhm/ Hair-like
organelles on a cell membrane that are shorter than *flagella*
and must be used en masse for locomotion or food
transfer; they are composed of ten pairs of *microtubules*
(especially [PROTISTA-CHROMALVEOLATA-
STRAMENOPILES-CILIOPHORA]).

CILIATED LOOP /**sil**-i-**ay**-tuhd .../ A *ciliated* organ of
probably sensory function on the anterior dorsal
epithelium of chaetognaths (CHAETOGNATHA).
Synonymous with "corona ciliata;" sometimes called
simply the *corona*.

CIRCULAR CANAL See *ring canal* (2).

CIRRUS /**seer**-ruhs/ **pl. cirri** /**seer**-ree/ 1. Any *tentacular* or
fibril-like projection. 2. Tuft-like *protist organelle* composed of
several joined *cilia* ([PROTISTA-CHROMALVEOLATA-
STRAMENOPILES-CILIOPHORA]). 3. An eversible male
copulatory organ of *flukes* and a few *flatworms*
(PLATYHELMINTHES especially -**Trematoda**). See also
penis. 4. Fleshy projection found on both the dorsal and
ventral sides of polychaete *parapodia* (ANNELIDA-
Polychaeta). 5. A feeding (*thoracic*) *appendage* of *barnacles*
(ARTHROPODA-CRUSTACEA-**Maxillopoda**-
Cirripedia). 6. One of several grasping structures used by
crinoids to cling to the substrate (ECHINODERMATA-
Crinoidea).

CIRRUS SAC /**seer**-ruhs …/ The structure used to hold the *fluke cirrus* (PLATYHELMINTHES-**Trematoda**).

CLAMS Common name for bivalves (mollusks with two-part *shells*), except for those with common names of their own, like cockles, geoducks, mussels, oysters, and scallops (MOLLUSCA-**Bivalvia**). See also *valve*.

CLEAVAGE /**klee**-vuj/ Early *embryonic* cell division, starting with the first division of the *zygote* to create two *blastomeres*, then four, eight, and so on.

CLITELLUM /kli-**te**-luhm/ In *earthworms* and other oligochaetes, the thick, *glandular* region of the body along *segments* 32 through 37, used in copulation and *cocoon* formation (ANNELIDA-**Oligochaeta**).

CLOACA /klo-**ay**-kah/ A single cavity that receives wastes from the *alimentary canal* and output from the reproductive system, as well as, where applicable, wastes from the *excretory* system. There is no specific term for the external opening of this orifice (it is not precisely an *anus*), but it is sometimes also referred to also as the cloaca, the *anus*, or the "cloacal opening" (for example ECHINODERMATA-**Holothuroidea**, NEMATODA). See also *rectum*.

CLOSED CIRCULATORY SYSTEM Any circulatory system in which the *blood* is completely enclosed in vessels, from the heart to the tissues and back (that is, has capillaries). Most invertebrate circulatory systems have a non-cellular lining, but the nemertean circulatory system is lined with "endothelium," a cellular matrix. In cephalopods and echinoderms the circulatory system is also lined with cells, but these are not *homologous* to the nemertean endothelium (ANNELIDA, BRACHIOPODA [probably], CHORDATA-CEPHALOCHORDATA,

ECHINODERMATA [highly reduced], MOLLUSCA-**Cephalopoda**, NEMERTEA, PHORONIDA; no circulatory system present in [ACANTHOCEPHALA], CNIDARIA, ECTOPROCTA, ENTOPROCTA [probably], NEMATODA, PLATYHELMINTHES, PORIFERA, ROTIFERA). See also *open circulatory system*.

CLYPEUS /**kliy**-pee-uhs/ In general, a medial *sclerite* or plate at the extreme anterior, such as between paired anterior *appendages* or structures (such as *antennae*, *chelicerae*, and *eyes*), and bearing the *labrum*; it is a commonly described part in insect taxonomy (ARTHROPODA, especially -HEXAPODA-**Insecta**, also -CHELICERATA-**Arachnida**, -CRUSTACEA).

CNIDA /**ni**-dah/ **pl. cnidae** /**ni**-dee/ See *cnidocyst*.

CNIDOBLAST /**ni**-do-blast/ See *cnidocyte*.

CNIDOCIL /**ni**-do-sil/ A small protrusion on a *cnidocyte*, which, when stimulated, causes the *cnidocyst* to discharge.

CNIDOCYST /**ni**-do-sist/ The cnidarian *organelle* of *cnycocytes* that contains a thread-like structure which, upon stimulation of the cell's *cnidocil*, is everted by rapid osmotic changes and attaches to its victim; different types of cnidocysts are characterized by the folding patterns of the thread and whether it is armed with barbs or adhesives; it can be considered a type of *extrusome*, although that term is more widely used with *protists* (CNIDARIA). Synonymous with "cnida." See also *nematocyst* (1), *ptychocyst*, and *spirocyst*.

CNIDOCYTE /**ni**-do-siyt/ A type of cell, unique to cnidarians, that has a *cnidocyst* (an *organelle* that shoots out a spiny or sticky thread when its *cnidocil* is stimulated); sometimes arranged in clumps, called "batteries"

(CNIDARIA). Synonymous with "nematocyte" and "cnidoblast."

CNIDOSACS /**ni**-do-saks/ Pouches on the ends of nudibranch *cerata* that contain the undigested *cnidocysts* the *animal* acquired from eating cnidarians (MOLLUSCA-**Gastropoda**-[NUDIBRANCHIA]).

COCCIDIOSIS /**kahk**-si-dee-o-suhs/ An *intestinal* disease in various vertebrates, including humans, caused by certain apicomplexan *protists* ([PROTISTA-CHROMALVEOLATA-STRAMENOPILES-APICOMPLEXA-CONOIDASIDA-COCCIDIASINA] for example -*Cryptosporidium*, -*Toxoplasma*, and others)

COCCOID /**kahk**-koyd/ Spherical.

COCOON /kuh-**koon**/ Any non-living case secreted or constructed by an *animal*, such as the *chitinous* container that holds *earthworm eggs* (ANNELIDA-**Oligochaeta**) or the *silk* enclosure of many insect *pupae* (ARTHROPODA-HEXAPODA-**Insecta**).

COELOM /**see**-lom/ This is a cavity that is derived from *mesoderm* and lies between the *alimentary canal* and the body wall; in it there are distinct organs and fluid, which move somewhat freely (as opposed to the organs being encased in a solid mass of cells); in addition, the inside of the cavity and all the organs in it are lined with a special tissue (*peritoneum*) and often muscle, both of which are also derived from *mesoderm*; *animals* that have a coelom are called "coelomate" (ANNELIDA, ARTHROPODA, BRACHIOPODA, CHAETOGNATHA, CHORDATA, ECHINODERMATA, ECTOPROCTA, HEMICHORDATA, MOLLUSCA, NEMERTEA, ONYCHOPHORA, PHORONIDA, PRIAPULIDA, TARDIGRADA). See also *acoelomate* and *pseudocoelomate*.

COELOMODUCT /see-**lo**-**mo**-duhkt/ Any tube derived mostly from *mesoderm* that connects the *coelomic* cavity to the outside; the end inside the *coelom* is *funnel*-shaped and lined with *cilia* that move certain things (usually *gametes* and/or *nitrogenous waste*) to the outside. Coelomoducts are paired and found on each *segment* in annelids, where they have been extensively studied and can be found merged with *nephridia* (ANNELIDA). In mollusks, they often connect the *pericardial cavity* to the *mantle cavity* (MOLLUSCA), and in onychophorans they lead from *coelomic* sacs to openings at the bases of the legs (ONYCHOPHORA).

COENOSARC /**see**-no-sahrk/ The *epidermis*, *mesoglea*, and *gastrodermis* of colonial hydrozoans, encased within the *perisarc* (CNIDARIA-**Hydrozoa**). Sometimes also used to describe the living tissue of *corals* and suggested for similar use in *bryozoans*.

COLLAGEN /**kah**-lah-jen/ A strong, gelatinous protein found in connective tissues.

COLLAR 1. In *choanocytes* and similar cells, the ring of interconnected *microvilli* that surrounds the *flagellum* (PORIFERA, [PROTISTA-OPISTHOKONTA-CHOANOMONADA]). 2. In hemichordates, a band of *coelom*-filled tissue that forms a lip around the base of the *proboscis* and precedes the *trunk* (HEMICHORDATA). Synonymous with "mesosome."

COLLAR CELL See *choanocyte*.

COLLOBLAST /**kah**-lo-blast/ In ctenophores, a specialized cell on the *epidermis* of the *tentacles* that makes sticky secretions useful for food capture (CTENOPHORA).

COLUMELLA /kahl-yoo-**mel**-lah/ The internal, central spire around which the gastropod *shell* spirals (MOLLUSCA-**Gastropoda**).

COMB ROW A longitudinal line of *ctenes* on the *epidermis* of ctenophores (CTENOPHORA).

COMMENSALISM /kah-**men**-sahl-i-zuhm/ An interspecific relationship in which one species benefits and the other gains no advantage nor suffers any disadvantage from the relationship. See also *symbiosis*.

COMPENSATION SAC In ectoprocts, the chamber that fills with seawater when the *polypide* is extended outside of the protective covering (ECTOPROCTA-**Gymnolaemata** for example -*Porella*, -*Micropoella*, -*Schizoporella*).

COMPLETE GUT An *alimentary canal* with a *mouth* and an *anus*; useful in having specialized regions for food treatment (e.g., grinding, storage, acidification, water reabsorption), since food passes each point only once (ANNELIDA, ARTHROPODA, BRACHIOPODA [except for **Articulata**], CHAETOGNATHA, CHORDATA, CYCLIOPHORA, ECHINODERMATA [except for **Ophiuroidea**], ECTOPROCTA, ENTOPROCTA, GASTROTRICHA, HEMICHORDATA, KINORHYNCHA, LORICIFERA, MOLLUSCA, NEMATODA, NEMERTEA, ONYCHOPHORA, PHORONIDA, PRIAPULIDA, ROTIFERA [usually], SIPUNCULA, TARDIGRADA). See also *anal pore*, as well as *incomplete gut*.

COMPLETE METAMORPHOSIS See *holometabolism*.

COMPOUND EYE *Photoreceptor* of arthropods that consists of several *ommatidia*; it has no lid and is covered with *exoskeleton* (ARTHROPODA).

CONJUGATION Complex mode of sexual reproduction in ciliates in which two similar *diploid* cells combine genetic material and become four *diploid* daughter cells ([PROTISTA-CHROMALVEOLATA-STRAMENOPILES-CILIOPHORA]). See also *micronucleus*.

CONTRACTILE VACUOLE /kuhn-**trak**-tiyl **vak**-yoo-ol/ A specialized *organelle*, found mainly in certain *protists*, used for *osmoregulation* and salt balance ([PROTISTA]).

COPULATORY SPICULES /**kahp**-yoo-lah-**tor**-ee **spik**-yoolz/ See *spicule* (2).

CORACIDIUM /kor-uh-**si**-di-yuhm/ In *tapeworms*, a special type of *oncosphere* where the *hexacanth* is encased in a single, *ciliated embryonic envelope* and is thus motile (PLATYHELMINTHES-**Cestoda**).

CORAL General term for anthozoans that are colonial and secrete a skeleton which is either proteinaceous ("soft corals," but see *organ-pipe coral*) or *calcareous* ("stony corals") (CNIDARIA-**Anthozoa** except, for example, **Hexacorallia**-<u>Actiniaria</u>). See also *sea anemones*.

CORONA /ko-**ro**-nah/ 1. The anterior end of a rotifer, bearing the *cilia* (ROTIFERA). Synonymous with "wheel organ." 2. Alternate term for the *ciliated loop* of chaetognaths (CHAETOGNATHA).

CORONA CILIATA /ko-**ro**-nah **sil**-ee-**ah**-tah/ See *ciliated loop*.

CORONATE LARVA /**ko**-ro-nayt …/ *Larval* type of gymnolaemate ectoprocts that brood their young; it is spherical and covered with rows of *cilia* (ECTOPROCTA-**Gymnolaemata**).

CORTEX /**kor**-teks/ The outer layer of *cytoplasm* in *heliozoans*. (In the similar-looking radiolarians— [PROTISTA-RHIZARIA-RADIOLARIA]—the outer capsule[s] of the *test* is referred to as the "cortical shell[s]."")

COSTA /**kaw**-stah/ 1. In some *protists*, an internal extension of the *flagellar* base ([PROTISTA-EXCAVATA-PARABASALIA]). 2. An extension of *sclerosepta* of *corals* that extends beyond the body wall of the living *polyp* (CNIDARIA-**Anthozoa-Hexacorallia**).

COXA /**kahk**-sah/ The *article* of an arthropod *appendage* that is closest to the body (ARTHROPODA).

CRAB Nebulous word that refers mostly to brachyuran decapods (ARTHROPODA-CRUSTACEA-**Malacostraca**-Decapoda-Brachyura), although anomuran decapods (-Anomura), xiphosurans (ARTHROPODA-CHELICERATA-**Merostomata**-Xiphosura), and some lice (ARTHROPODA-HEXAPODA-**Insecta**-Phthiraptera-Anoplura-*Phthirus-pubis*) are also called crabs.

CROCHETS /kro-**shays**/ Microscopic hooks on *caterpillar prolegs*; they are *sclerotized* and organized into circles or rows, and they are used to assist the *caterpillar* in holding on to surfaces (ARTHROPODA-HEXAPODA-**Insecta**-Lepidoptera).

CROP In both insects and annelids, the section of the *alimentary canal* after the *esophagus* and before the *gizzard*, used in the storage and crushing of food (ARTHROPODA-HEXAPODA-**Insecta**, ANNELIDA).

CRYPTOZOITE /krip-to-**zo**-iyt/ In the *Plasmodium* (*malaria*) life cycle, the stage that follows the *sporozoite* and resides in the liver cells. It eventually becomes a *schizont*, and, via *schizogony*, becomes either more cryptozoites or *merozoites* ([PROTISTA-CHROMALVEOLATA-STRAMENOPILES-APICOMPLEXA-ACONOIDASIDA-HAEMOSPORORIDA]-*Plasmodium*).

CRYSTALLINE STYLE /**kris**-tah-leen …/ In some mollusks, the gelatinous rod secreted at the juncture between the *stomach* and *intestine*; it is rotated by *cilia* and secretes digestive enzymes (MOLLUSCA-**Bivalvia**, -**Gastropoda**, -**Monoplacophora**). See also *protostyle*.

CTENE /teen/ A short row of large *cilia* that makes a comb-like structure used in rows (*comb rows*) for locomotion in ctenophorans (CTENOPHORA). Synonymous with "comb." See also *membranelle* and *undulating membrane*.

CTENIDIA /tuh-**nid**-ee-ah/ Name for the *gill* structures of mollusks (MOLLUSCA).

CUTICLE /**kyoo**-ti-kuhl/ Any non-living covering produced by *ectodermal* tissues (usually the *epidermis* but also the *epithelium* of the arthropod *foregut* and *hindgut*) (ANNELIDA, ARTHROPODA, NEMATODA, NEMATOMORPHA, ONYCHOPHORA).

CUVIERIAN TUBULES /kyoo-**ver**-ee-ahn …/ In *sea cucumbers*, the sticky, thread-like structures found between the *respiratory tree* and its connection to the *cloaca*; they are everted out of the "*anus*" for defense (ECHINODERMATA-**Holothuroidea**).

CYDIPPID LARVA /siy-**dip**-pid …/ The *larva* of ctenophores (CTENOPHORA).

CYPHONAUTES LARVA /**siy**-fo-**naw**-teez …/ *Larval* type of gymnolaemate ectoprocts that does not brood its young; it is triangular, flattened, and covered with rows of *cilia*, and it has an *alimentary canal*; it sometimes has a *chitinous* shell with two *valves* (ECTOPROCTA-**Gymnolaemata**).

CYST /sist/ **adj. encysted** /en-**sis**-ted/ Any protective covering that contains a dormant organism, or the life cycle stage during which an organism becomes inactive while in a protective covering. See also *encyst* and *excyst*.

CYSTICERCUS /**sis**-ti-**ser**-kuhs/ *Larval* stage in *tapeworms* in which the organism is dormant in the muscle of the *intermediate host*; this stage occurs after the *oncosphere larva* (the enveloped *hexacanth*) and is the one that grows into the *adult* after ingestion by the *definitive host* (PLATYHELMINTHES-**Cestoda**). Synonymous with "bladder worm." See also *hydatid*.

CYTOPLASM /**siy**-to-**pla**-zuhm/ The contents of a cell membrane, with the exception of the nucleus.

CYTOPROCT /**siy**-to-prahkt/ The location through which undigested materials pass through the *pellicle* and out of the *cytoplasm* of some *protists* ([PROTISTA-CHROMALVEOLATA-STRAMENOPILES-CILIOPHORA]).

CYTOSTOME /**siy**-to-stom/ The *organelle* of ciliates through which food enters to make a food vacuole ([PROTISTA-CHROMALVEOLATA-STRAMENOPILES-CILIOPHORA]).

D, E

DACTYLOZOOID /dak-ti-luh-**zo**-id/ In colonial
hydrozoans, a *polyp* that is specialized for defense
(CNIDARIA-**Hydrozoa**).

DADDY LONGLEGS A common name for any long-
and thin-legged arthropod, often referring to certain
spiders (ARTHROPODA-CHELICERATA-
Arachnida-Araneae), but most commonly referring to
certain *harvestmen* (ARTHROPODA-CHELICERATA-
Arachnida-Opiliones-Eupnoi). Also written as "daddy
long legs" or "daddy-long-legs."

DART SAC Reproductive structure in some land *snails* that
shoots the *love dart* (a sharp, hardened, delivery device for
fertilization-related chemicals) into a mating partner
(MOLLUSCA-**Gastropoda**-[PULMONATA]). See also
bursa copulatrix and *hypodermic impregnation.*

DEFINITIVE HOST The host where a *parasite* engages in
sexual reproduction. Also called the "primary host" or
"final host." See also *intermediate host.*

DELAMINATION /**dee**-lam-i-**nay**-shuhn/ A mode of
gastrulation in which *blastomeres* divide to form a layer of
cells on the inside of the *blastula*, the inside layer
becoming the *endoderm.*

DEPOSIT FEEDING Feeding on *benthic detritus*. "Direct" deposit feeders eat their way through the substrate, and "indirect" deposit feeders spread out *tentacles* to bring food from the surface to their *mouth*.

DERIVED Describing a trait that has been modified through evolution such that it does not resemble the *ancestral* condition.

DETERMINATE DEVELOPMENT Type of development where the *blastomeres* irreversibly differentiate starting from the first division of the *zygote*. See also *eutely*, *indeterminate development*, and *spiral cleavage*.

DETORSION /dee-**tor**-zhuhn/ In some mollusks, a process by which the internal arrangement of organs converts back to state in which the *mantle cavity* is posterior (MOLLUSCA-**Gastropoda** especially -[NUDIBRANCHIA]). See also *torsion*.

DETRITUS /dee-**triy**-tis/ The particulate debris of dead organisms, found on the ground, sea floor, or other substrate, or floating in the water or air.

DEUTEROCEREBRUM /**doo**-tur-o-sur-**ree**-bruhm/ The part of the arthropod brain that innervates the *antennae* (ARTHROPODA-CRUSTACEA, -HEXAPODA, -MYRIAPODA). See also *protocerebrum* and *tritocerebrum*.

DEUTEROSTOME /**doo**-tuhr-o-stom/ **adj.** **deuterostomatous** /du-tuhr-o-**stom**-ah-tus/ A *triploblastic animal* that has a type of *embryological* development in which the *blastopore* becomes the *anus* (ECHINODERMATA, HEMICHORDATA, CHORDATA). See also *protostome*.

DEUTOMERITE /doo-to-**mer**-iyt/ In gregarines that *parasitize* insects and crustaceans, the most posterior part of the cell, which contains the nucleus ([PROTISTA-CHROMALVEOLATA-STRAMENOPILES-

APICOMPLEXA-CONOIDASIDA-
GREGARINASINA]). See also *epimerite* and *protomerite*.

DEXTRAL /**deks**-trahl/ Meaning "right-handed," it
describes gastropod shells that have their opening to the
right of the *columella* when held with the apex (smallest
whorls) up and the opening facing the observer
(MOLLUSCA-**Gastropoda**).

DIGENETIC /**diy**-ge-**ne**-tik/ Describing *flukes* that
have both an *intermediate host* and a *definitive host*
(PLATYHELMINTHES-**Trematoda**).

DIGESTIVE CECUM /… **see**-kuhm/ See *pyloric cecum*.

DIGESTIVE GLAND 1. Any organ or patch of cells that
secretes enzymes useful in digestion. 2. See *pyloric cecum*.

DIOECIOUS /diy-**ee**-shuhs/ Describing species that have
separate male and female individuals. See also *monoecious*.

DIPLEURULA /diy-**ploor**-yoo-lah/ The first type of
echinoderm *larva*; it has one band of *cilia*
(ECHINODERMATA).

DIPLOBLASTIC /dip-lo-**blas**-tik/ Describing *embryos* with
only two *germ layers*, *ectoderm* and *endoderm* (and describing
any individual that develops from such an *embryo* or any
taxon descended from such an ancestor). This has been
the condition traditionally ascribed to the cnidarians and
ctenophores (CNIDARIA, CTENOPHORA), although
cells in their *mesoglea* may indicate they are *triploblastic*. It is
debatable whether *sponges* (PORIFERA) truly *gastrulate* and
differentiate *germ layers*.

DIPLOID /**dip**-loyd/ **n. diploidy** /**dip**-loy-dee/ Describing
cells or organisms that have two copies of each
chromosome; these copies are usually obtained from two

parents, and thus they often have different versions of each gene. See also *haploid* and *polyploid*, as well as *homologous*.

DIRECT DEVELOPMENT See *hemimetabolism*.

DIVERTICULUM /diy-vur-**tik**-yoo-luhm/ Any blind sac branching off of an anatomical tract (that is, a *cecum*) or body cavity, especially off the *alimentary canal*. See also *antrum*, *atrium*, *bursa*, *lumen*, and *sinus*.

DOLIOLARIA /**do**-lee-o-**leyr**-ee-ah/ In *sea cucumbers*, the *larval* stage immediately after the *auricularia* stage; it is cylindrical and has five transverse bands of *cilia* (ECHINODERMATA-**Holothuroidea**). See also *pentacula* and *vitellaria*.

DORSAL VALVE The hardened plate that covers the dorsal side of brachiopods (BRACHIOPODA).

DUO-GLAND SYSTEM /**doo**-o-gland …/ Generally used to refer to an adhesion and locomotory system in which one or more sets of *epidermal* cells secretes adhesive substances (the "adhesion *gland*") and another set or sets of cells secretes substances to break down those adhesives (the "releasing *gland*") (ECHINODERMS [in *tube feet*], especially PLATYHELMINTHES).

EARTHWORMS A class of common, terrestrial annelids (ANNELIDA-**Oligochaeta**).

ECDYSIS /ek-**diy**-sis/ Stage of arthropod *molting* during which the *animal* swells with water and (in some cases) air, and the old *exoskeleton* splits and is removed from the body (ARTHROPODA). See also *anecdysis*, *metecdysis*, and *proecdysis*.

ECDYSONE /ek-**diy**-son/ In insects, crustaceans, and other arthropods, the hormone that directly affects the *epidermal* cells during *molting* (ARTHROPODA).

ECDYSOZOA /ek-**diy**-so-**zo**-ah/ *Protostome* clade containing those phyla that usually *molt* (ARTHROPODA, CHAETOGNATHA, LORICIFERA, KINORHYNCHA, NEMATODA, NEMATOMORPHA, ONYCHOPHORA, PRIAPULIDA, TARDIGRADA). See also *ecdysone*.

ECHINOPLUTEUS /ee-**kiy**-no-**ploo**-tee-uhs/ The *larval* stage of echinoids that is after the *pluteus* stage and characterized by long *arms*; it resembles the *ophiopluteus larva* of ophiuroids (ECHINODERMATA-**Echinoidea**).

ECTODERM /**ek**-to-derm/ The outer *embryonic* layer of cells.

ECTOLECITHAL /**ek**-to-**les**-i-thahl/ Type of *egg* that has *yolk* deposited on the outside of the cell (especially PLATYHELMINTHES-[LECITHOEPITHELIATA], -**Neoophora**).

ECTOPLASM /**ek**-to-**pla**-suhm/ The firm outer layer of the *cytoplasm* of amoebas ([PROTISTA-AMOEBOZOA]). Synonymous with "gel."

EFFERENT /**ef**-fer-ent/ Directed or conducting away from, as opposed to *afferent*.

EGESTION /ee-**ges**-chuhn/ The elimination of undigested materials from an organism.

EGG 1. The immobile, female, typically *haploid* cell that usually joins with a mobile *sperm* to create a new organism. Synonymous with "ovum." 2. An *encysted embryo* and *yolk*, capable of living away from the parent. See also *gamete* and *gonad*.

EJACULATORY DUCT /ee-**jak**-yoo-lah-**to**-ree …/ Any tube that carries *sperm* and secretions from the *seminal vesicle* to the *cloaca* or *urethra*.

ELYTRA /ee-**liy**-trah/ The hardened forewings of *beetles* (ARTHROPODA-HEXAPODA-**Insecta**-Coleoptera).

EMBRYO A general term for an organism in the early stages of development, especially when basic tissue layers are formed and the fundamental organ systems and body plan are being determined; it may also refer to more advanced stages of development in organisms (such as in humans) where one does not traditionally refer to a *larva* or a *larval* form with a special term.

EMBRYONIC ENVELOPE One of two *syncytial* coatings of the *hexacanth larva*; the outer envelope does not usually persist through the entire *hexacanth* stage (PLATYHELMINTHES-**Cestoda**). See also *oncosphere*.

ENCRUSTING Low and in contact with the substrate, commonly used to refer to a type of ectoproct colony (ECTOPROCTA, for example *Membranipora*). See also *arborescent* and *stoloniferous*.

ENCYST /en-**sist**/ To become encased in a *cyst* (the opposite of *excyst*).

ENDITE /**en**-diyt/ Generally, any inner lobe of a crustacean *appendage* that arises from the *protopodite* (ARTHROPODA-CRUSTACEA). See also *exite*, *biramous*.

ENDODERM/**en**-do-durm/ The layer of *embryonic* cells that lines the inside of the *gastrula* and subsequent *embryonic* stages; this layer becomes the lining of the *alimentary canal* and can give rise to particular organs.

ENDOLECITHAL /**en**-do-**le**-si-thahl/ Type of *egg* that has the *yolk* on the inside of the *cytoplasm* (especially PLATYHELMINTHES-**Turbellaria**-[ARCHOPHORA]).

ENDOPLASM /**en**-do-**pla**-zuhm/ 1. The *cytoplasm* inside the *ectoplasm* ([PROTISTA-AMOEBOZOA]). Synonymous with "sol." 2. In radiolarians, the *cytoplasm* inside the *central capsule* ([PROTISTA-RHIZARIA-RADIOLARIA]). Synonymous with "intracapsular cytoplasm;" see also *calymma*.

ENDOPODITE /**en**-do-**po**-diyt/ The inner (more ventral) branch (*ramus*) of an arthropod *biramous appendage*, which arises from the distal end of the *protopodite* (ARTHROPODA). See also *biramous, exopodite*.

ENDOSTYLE /**en**-do-stiyl/ *Ciliated* groove on the dorsal side of the *pharynx* of tunicates; it produces a sheet of mucous that captures food (CHORDATA-TUNICATA).

ENTEROCOELY /**en**-ter-o-**see**-lee/ A mode of *coelom* formation in *embryos* whereby it arises from outpocketings of the *archenteron* (DEUTEROSTOMIA). See *schizocoely*.

ENTOCODON /en-to-**ko**-dahn/ The mass of cells on the end of a hydrozoan *medusa bud* that becomes the *velum* and *subumbrellar surface* (CNIDARIA-**Hydrozoa**).

EPHYRA /e-**fiy**-rah/ An immature *medusa* after separating from the *scyphistoma* (CNIDARIA-**Cubozoa**, -**Scyphozoa**).

EPIBOLY /ee-**pi**-bo lee/ A method of *gastrulation* in *yolky eggs* in which the *micromeres* at the *animal pole* multiply and cover the *macromeres* at the *vegetal pole*, engulfing the *macromeres*, which then become *endoderm*. The ring where the *micromeres* and *macromeres* meet becomes the lip of the *blastopore*, and cells destined to become the *mesoderm* migrate in from this point.

EPICUTICLE /e-pee-**kyoo**-ti-kuhl/ The waxy outer layer of the arthropod *exoskeleton* (ARTHROPODA).

EPIDERMIS /e-pee-**duhr**-mis/ The outer layer of cells of an organism. See also *hypodermis*.

EPIMERITE /e-pee-**mer**-iyt/ In gregarines that *parasitize* insects and crustaceans, the most anterior part of the cell, which attaches to the *alimentary canal* of the host ([PROTISTA-CHROMALVEOLATA-STRAMENOPILES-APICOMPLEXA-CONOIDASIDA-GREGARINASINA]). See also *deutomerite* and *protomerite*.

EPIPODITE /e-pee-**po**-diyt/ The most distal *exite* of a crustacean *appendage*; more proximal *exites* are often called "pre-epipodites" (ARTHROPODA-CRUSTACEA). See also *biramous*.

EPITHELIUM /e-pee-**thee**-lee-uhm/ Type of tissue in which cells, many of which are secretory, are tightly packed in a thin layer that covers organs or lines ducts and sacs.

EPITOKE /e-pee-toke/ 1. The reproductive (swarming) stage in the life cycle of many nereid polychaetes; it has larger *eyes* and *parapodia* than the non-reproductive morphology (MOLLUSCA-**Polychaeta**-Nereidae). 2. The sexual worm formed by the transverse fission of syllid polychaetes (MOLLUSCA-**Polychaeta**-Syllidae). 3. The *gamete*-containing, detached, posterior end of eunicid polychaetes (MOLLUSCA-**Polychaeta**-Eunicidae).

ESOPHAGUS Any tube carrying food to the *stomach*.

EUKARYOTIC /yoo-**kar**-ee-**ah**-tik/ Having membrane-bound *organelles*, especially the nucleus.

EUTELY /**yoo**-te-lee/ Condition in which the number of cells in certain tissues, or even the whole body, is the same for all members of a species across their entire *adult* lives; once ascribed to all *pseudocoelomates*, it is now known, to some degree, in a variety of groups; also, in nematodes, which were famous for strict eutely of the entire body, variation has been demonstrated in the number of cells in their *epidermis* (especially, but with exceptions [ACANTHOCEPHALA], ANNELIDA [certain larvae and tissues], CHORDATA-TUNICATA-**Appendicularia**, DICYEMIDA, GASTROTRICHA, NEMATODA [most cell lineages], PLATYHELMINTHES, ROTIFERA, TARDIGRADA).

EXCRETION The process by which *nitrogenous waste* is eliminated from the body.

EXCURRENT SIPHON or EXCURRENT CANAL /eks-kur-rent .../ In *leuconoid sponges*, a canal that carries water from inner *flagellated chambers* through the *osculum* and out of the body (PORIFERA). See *atrial siphon/canal* for tunicates, see *exhalant siphon/canal* for mollusks.

EXCYST /ek-**sist**/ **n. excystation** /ek-sis-**tay**-shun/ To emerge from a *cyst* (the opposite of *encyst*).

EXHALANT SIPHON or EXHALANT CANAL /eks-**hay**-lant .../ The tube of tissue through which water and wastes leave the *mantle cavity* of bivalves (MOLLUSCA-**Bivalvia**). See *atrial siphon/canal* for tunicates and *excurrent siphon/canal* for sponges.

EXITE /**eks**-iyt/ Generally, any outer lobe of a crustacean *appendage* that arises from the *protopodite*, such as an *epipodite* (ARTHROPODA-CRUSTACEA). See also *endite*, *biramous*.

EXOPODITE /**eks**-o-**po**-diyt/ The outer (more dorsal or lateral) branch (*ramus*) of a *biramous appendage*, which arises from the distal end of the *protopodite* (ARTHROPODA). See also *biramous*, *endopodite*.

EXOSKELETON /**eks**-o-**ske**-le-tuhn/ The complex outer covering of arthropods secreted by the *epidermis*; it is divided into two main layers: outer *epicuticle* made of protein, waxes, and fats, and inner *procuticle* containing *chitin* and other substances (ARTHROPODA).

EXTENSORS /eks-**ten**-suhrz/ Muscle fibers in arthropods that return the *abdomen* to its usual extended position; they are much smaller than *flexors* (ARTHROPODA especially -CRUSTACEA).

EXTRACAPSULAR CYTOPLASM /eks-trah-**kap**-soo-lahr **siy**-to-**plaz**-uhm/ See *calymma*.

EXTRACAPSULUM /eks-trah-**kap**-soo-luhm/ See *calymma*.

EXTRUSOME /**eks**-troo-som/ An *organelle* that, with the proper stimulation, will release its contents to the outside, sometimes explosively; commonly used with *protists* but also an accurate term for such structures in *metazoans*, such as for the *cnidocysts* of cnidarians; there are many different types, distinguished by variations in microstructure; examples also include *haptocysts*, *nematocysts* (2), and *trichocysts*.

EXUMBRELLA /**eks**-uhm-**brel**-lah/ The side of a *medusa* opposite the *mouth* (CNIDARIA-**Cubozoa**, -**Hydrozoa**, -**Scyphozoa**). Synonymous with "aboral" in *jellyfish*.

EYE Any light-sensing organ, especially those with a with a lens, pupil (aperture through which light passes), or other image-enhancing structure. See also *compound eye*, *eyespot*, and *ocellus*.

EYESPOT 1. A light-sensing structure that consists of a pigmented area and an underlying layer of light-sensitive cells; it lacks a lens or pupil (an aperture through which light passes); the word can sometimes refer to just the visible aggregation of pigment, the cast shadow of which gives information on the direction of a light source. 2. Sometimes used for *stigma*, which is a subcellular structure that performs the same function in *protists*. 3. A false *eye* formed in the surface patterns of some *animals*; it frightens or confuses potential predators.

EYESTALK Any combination of an *eye* at the end of a *stalk*, common in crustaceans (especially ARTHROPODA-CRUSTACEA).

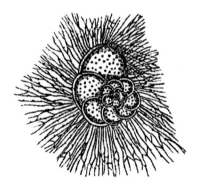

F, G

FANGS 1. The modified *chelicerae* of spiders (ARTHROPODA-CHELICERATA-**Arachnida**-Araneae). 2. The poison-containing *appendages* on the first *trunk segment* of centipedes (ARTHROPODA-MYRIAPODA-**Chilopoda**). Synonymous with "forcipule" and "poison claws" in centipedes.

FECES /**fee**-seez/ Waste material eliminated from the *alimentary canal*. See also *frass*.

FILARIFORM LARVA /fi-**leyr**-i-form …/ A nematode *larva* that follows the *rhabditiform* (feeding) *larva* and is the infective stage; it has an *esophagus* and a *mouth*, but the *mouth* is closed (NEMATODA for example -*Necator-americanus*).

FILIFORM TENTACLES /**fi**-li-form …/ Long, thin *tentacles* of hydrozoan *polyps*, which usually have an even covering of *cnidocytes* (CNIDARIA-**Hydrozoa**). See also *capitate tentacles*.

FILOPODIUM /fi-lo-**po**-di-uhm/ A thread-like *pseudopodium* of certain *protists* that is composed of *ectoplasm* and *microfilament* supports ([PROTISTA]).

FILTER-FEEDING Obtaining food by passing water through a network of openings that trap everything above a certain size; while most filter-feeders eat only microorganisms and *detritus, basket stars*

(ECHINODERMATA-**Ophiuroidea**) can trap larger debris and organisms.

FIN Any extension of the body that forms a flat structure used in stabilization or locomotion (for example CHAETOGNATHA).

FLAGELLATED CHAMBER /**fla**-jel-**lay**-ted …/ In *sponges*, an internal cavity that is lined with *choanocytes*; also called a *radial canal* in *syconoid sponges*; sometimes referred to as a "choanocyte chamber" (PORIFERA).

FLAGELLUM /fla-**gel**-luhm/ **pl. flagella** /fla-**gel**-ah/ **adj. flagellar** /fla-**gel**-lahr/ A string-like *organelle* used alone or in groups for locomotion. It is on the surface of many different kind of cells and is composed of ten pairs of *microtubules*. Common in *protists*, it is also used by the *sperm* cells of most taxa, as well as the *choanocytes* of *sponges*.

FLAME BULB A modified *flame cell* that has multiple *cilia* and the nucleus located away from *cilia* bases; also used to describe a multicellular aggregation of *flame cells* at the *coelomic* end of a *protonephridium*.

FLAME CELL An *ectodermally* derived cell used for *osmoregulation* in several phyla, located at the *coelomic* end of a *nephridium* (whether a *funnel* or closed); in its simplest form, it consists of a cup of *cytoplasm* with one long *cilium* at the bottom, surrounded by *microvilli*, and with the nucleus near the base of the *cilium*; more complicated forms are called *flame bulbs* and *solenocytes*; aggregations of flame cells in *protonephridia* are sometimes also called *flame bulbs*. See also *renette cell*.

FLATWORM Any platyhelminth, especially a turbellarian (PLATYHELMINTHES especially -**Turbellaria**).

FLEAS Insects in the order Siphonaptera, so named for their sucking mouthparts ("siphon") and wingless bodies ("aptera") (ARTHROPODA-HEXAPODA-**Insecta**-Siphonaptera).

FLEXORS /**fleks**-orz/ Muscle fibers in arthropods that pull the *abdomen* toward the *cephalothorax*, often propelling the *animal* backwards; they are much larger than *extensors* (ARTHROPODA especially -CRUSTACEA).

FLUKE /flook/ Common name for a trematode flatworm (PLATYHELMINTHES-**Trematoda**).

FOOD POUCH One of eight pockets along the outer rim of scyphozoan *medusae* to which *cilia* carry food to be picked up by the *oral arms* and taken to the *mouth* (CNIDARIA-**Scyphozoa**). Not synonymous with *stomach pouch* or *gastric pouch*.

FOOT 1. The structure found on the ventral side of mollusks that consists primarily of muscle and is modified for locomotion, food gathering, and digging (MOLLUSCA). 2. The posterior end of rotifers (ROTIFERA).

FORCIPULE /**for**-si-pyool/ See *fangs* (2).

FOREGUT /**for**-guht/ Used mostly for arthropods, this is the anterior end of the *alimentary canal*, specialized for the ingestion and storage of food. The foregut and the *hindgut* are *ectodermally* derived and lined with *cuticle* (ARTHROPODA). See also *midgut*.

FOUNDER CELL In *sponges*, the *spicule*-producing cell (*scleroblast*) that determines the shape of a new *spicule* (PORIFERA). See also *thickener cell*.

FRASS /fras/ Insect *feces* (ARTHROPODA-HEXAPODA-**Insecta**).

FUNICULUS /fyoo-**nik**-yoo-luhs/ 1. Any bundle of fibers.
2. In ectoprocts, the cord that connects the *alimentary canal* and *ovary* of a *zooid* to the body wall; it also gives rise to the new *alimentary canal* after the *brown body* forms (ECTOPROCTA).

FUNNEL 1. Generally used for any structure in the shape of a tapering tube (e.g., the "sperm funnel" in annelids); most commonly used for certain structures associated with the *excretory* system (e.g., "nephridial funnel") (especially ANNELIDA, BRACHIOPODA). 2. The tubular opening of the *mantle cavity* in cephalopods used for generating a stream of water used in locomotion (i.e., jet propulsion) and, in the face of danger, quickly making an ink cloud upon exit (MOLLUSCA-**Cephalopoda**). See also *ink sac.*

FUNNEL ORGAN Name for the set of distinct, separate pads on the inside of a cephalopod *funnel*, hypothesized to be *glandular* in function (MOLLUSCA-**Cephalopoda**). Synonymous with "organ of Verrill" (and variations).

FURCA /**fur**-kah/ **pl. furcae** /**fur**-kee/ **or furcas** /**fur**-kahz/
1. Generally, any forked *appendage*, organ, or structure.
2. Most notably, in springtails it is the long, forked *appendage* that arises from the ventral side of the fourth *abdominal segment* and which is held beneath the body under tension until needed to catapult the *animal* several centimeters away (ARTHROPODA-HEXAPODA-**Entognatha**-**Collembola**). Synonymous in use as the diminutive, "furcula."

FURCULA /**fur**-kyoo-lah/ See *furca.*

GAMETE /**ga**-meet/ General term for an *egg* (*ovum*) or *sperm* cell; these are typically *haploid* and able to unite with another gamete to form a *diploid* cell (the *zygote*), which develops into a new individual. See also *gonad*.

GAMETOCYTE /ga-**mee**-to-siyt/ See *gamont*.

GAMONT /**ga**-mahnt/ A life cycle stage of some *protists*, following the *trophozoite*, that gives rise to *gametes*; "microgamonts" (= "microgametocytes") produce "microgametes" (*sperm*), and "macrogamonts" (= "macrogametocytes") give rise to "macrogametes" (*ova*); in species with *syzygy*, where gamonts join before *gamete* production, the cluster of joined gamonts is also referred to as a gamont ([PROTISTA]). Synonymous with "gametocyte."

GANGLION /**gang**-li-ahn/ Any aggregation of nerve cells.

GASTER /**gas**-tur/ Although generally referring to a *stomach* or, as an adjective (*gastric*), describing things associated with the *alimentary canal*, it is most commonly and accurately used to refer to the enlarged posterior *abdomen* of thin-waisted hymenopteran insects (ants, bees, and wasps: ARTHROPODA-HEXAPODA-**Insecta**-Hymenoptera). This is because the thin waist of these insects does not separate the *thorax* from the *abdomen* exactly, and some *abdominal* segments are tightly associated with the *thorax*; thus, the usual insect structure—head, *thorax*, and *abdomen*—has limited utility in describing these insects.

GASTRIC CECUM /**gas**-trik **see**-kuhm/ See *diverticulum*.

GASTRIC FILAMENT /**gas**-trik **fil**-ah-ment/ See *mesenteric filament*.

GASTRIC MILL /**gas**-trik …/ In crustaceans, the grinding apparatus in the *cardiac stomach*, which is formed by three *chitinous* teeth that project into the *stomach* (ARTHROPODA-CRUSTACEA).

GASTRIC POUCH /**gas**-trik …/ In scyphozoan *medusae*, one of four sacs off the sides of the *stomach* in which food is digested (CNIDARIA-**Scyphozoa**). Synonymous with "stomach pouch." Not synonymous with *food pouch*.

GASTRODERMIS /**gas**-tro-**der**-mis/ In cnidarians, the layer of cells rising from the *endoderm* that lines the inside the *alimentary canal*, starting at the *mouth* (CNIDARIA). This term is sometimes used to refer to the *endoderm* in general.

GASTROLITH /**gas**-tro-lith/ A deposit of calcium salts made in the *stomach* of many crustaceans before molting (during *proecdysis*) to store calcium needed later to harden the new *exoskeleton* (ARTHROPODA-CRUSTACEA).

GASTROVASCULAR CAVITY /**gas**-tro-**vas**-kyoo-luhr …/ Alternative term for the *alimentary canal* of cnidarians and ctenophores (CNIDARIA, CTENOPHORA).

GASTROZOOID /**gas**-tro-**zo**-id/ Hydrozoan *polyp* that is capable of feeding independently (CNIDARIA-**Hydrozoa**).

GASTRULA /**gas**-troo-lah/ The *embryonic* stage following the segregation of the *germ layers* (*gastrulation*) in the *blastula*, and which usually has a primitive *alimentary canal* (*archenteron* and *blastopore*). See also *stereogastrula*.

GASTRULATION /**gas**-troo-**lay**-shuhn/ The process by which a *blastula* separates its *germ layers* and usually forms an *archenteron* and *blastopore*, becoming a *gastrula*; this can occur in five different ways: *delamination*, *epiboly*, *ingression*, *invagination*, or *involution*.

GEL /jel/ See *ectoplasm*.

GEMMULE /**jem**-myool/ A *cyst*-like *bud* made in the *mesohyl* of fresh-water *sponges* that can survive desiccation; it is made by, and is filled with, several *amoebocytes* and is covered with a protective coat composed of *collagen* and *spicules* (PORIFERA-**Demospongiae**-Spongillidae). See also *amphidisk*.

GENITAL BURSAE /... **bur**-see/ Found at the bases of the *arms* of *brittle stars*, these sacs open to the outside and have the *gonads* on the *coelomic* sides of their walls; they are also used in respiration (ECHINODERMATA-**Ophiuroidea**). See also *bursa*.

GERM CELL A *gamete* (*sperm* or *egg*) or one of the cells from which it arises.

GERMINAL CELL Generally, any cell that gives rise to other cells.

GERM LAYERS The layers of cells in the early *embryo*— *ectoderm*, *endoderm*, and sometimes *mesoderm*—which differentiate during *gastrulation* and give rise to different body regions and organ systems.

GIARDIASIS /jee-ahr-**diy**-uh-sis/ Common ailment of the *intestines* in humans (and many other vertebrates) caused by *flagellated protists* in the genus *Giardia*; infection is caused by   the ingestion of *cysts*, which give rise to motile *trophozoites* ([PROTISTA-EXCAVATA-FORNICATA-EOPHARYNGIA-DIPLOMONADIDA-GIARDIINAE]-*Giardia*).

GILL Any structure used for gas exchange in water.

GILL CLEANER The extended *epipodite* of a *crab maxilliped*, especially the first one, used to remove debris from the *gills* (ARTHROPODA-CRUSTACEA-**Malacostraca**-Decapoda-Brachyura).

GILL SLITS See *pharyngeal slits*.

GIRDLE /**gur**-duhl/ 1. The ridge of *mantle* encircling the *foot* and *gills* in *chitons* (MOLLUSCA-**Polyplacophora**). 2. The groove containing the transverse *flagellum* in dinoflagellates when that groove is not spiraled ([PROTISTA-CHROMALVEOLATA-ALVEOLATA-DINOZOA-DINOFLAGELLATA]). See also *annulus* and *sulcus*.

GIZZARD /**gi**-zurd/ A section of the *alimentary canal* specialized for grinding food; it follows the *crop* and is commonly found in annelids and arthropods (ANNELIDA, ARTHROPODA).

GLADIUS /**gla**-dee-uhs/ The *chitinous*, internal structure of many squids, which is shaped like a spear point and located inside the dorsal surface of the *mantle* (MOLLUSCA-**Cephalopoda**-Decapodiformes, -Octopodiformes-Vampyromorphida-*Vampyroteuthis-infernalis*). Synonymous with "pen."

GLAND Any organ that has the primary function of producing and secreting an important chemical (or chemicals).

GLOCHIDIUM /glo-**kid**-ee-uhm/ A modified *veliger larva* of some freshwater bivalves; it attaches to the *gills* or bodies of fish where it *encysts*, develops, and eventually emerges as a *juvenile clam* (MOLLUSCA-**Bivalvia**-**Palaeoheterodonta**-Unionoida-Unionidae).

GNATHOBASES /**nath**-o-bay-sez/ The bristled bases of *horseshoe crab* legs, which are used to purée food before it enters the *mouth* (ARTHROPODA-CHELICERATA-**Merostomata** [which, appropriately, means "thigh mouth"] -Xiphosura).

GNATHOPODS /**nath**-o-pahdz/ The *subchelate* second and third *thoracic appendages* of male amphipods (ARTHROPODA-CRUSTACEA-Malacostraca-**AMPHIPODA**).

GONAD /**go**-nad/ General term for an *ovary* or *testis*; that is, an organ that makes *gametes* (*ova* and/or *sperm*).

GONODUCT /**gah**-no-duhkt/ Any duct that generally transfers *eggs* or *sperm*.

GONOPHORE /**gah**-no-for/ A highly modified hydrozoan *medusa* that remains attached to the *polyp* and produces *gametes* there (CNIDARIA-**Hydrozoa**). See also *sporosac*.

GONOPORE /**gah**-no-por/ Any opening between the reproductive system and the outside.

GONOTHECA /gah-no-**thee**-kah/ The *perisarc* of a colonial hydrozoan that covers a *blastostyle* (the reproductive extension of the *coenosarc*) to make the *gonozooid* (CNIDARIA-**Hydrozoa**).

GONOZOOID /gah-no-**zo**-id/ In colonial hydrozoans, the *polyp* type that is specialized for making *medusae* or *gametes*; it consists of a *blastostyle* surrounded by a *gonotheca* (CNIDARIA-**Hydrozoa**).

GORDIAN WORMS /**gor**-dee-ahn .../ Common name for nematomorphs, also called "hairworms" or "horsehair worms" (NEMATOMORPHA).

GRASPING SPINES Four to 14 *chitinous* spines on the heads of chaetognaths, used in prey capture (CHAETOGNATHA).

GREEN GLAND See *antennal gland*.

GRUB /gruhb/ A plump, pale, soft, insect (especially *beetle*) *larva* with *thoracic legs* (ARTHROPODA-HEXAPODA-**Insecta** especially -Coleoptera).

GUT See *alimentary canal*.

GYNECOPHORAL GROOVE /giy-nee-**kaw**-fuhr-ahl …/ In *Schistosoma flukes*, the longitudinal groove along the body of the male by which he holds the female during copulation (PLATYHELMINTHES-**Trematoda**-*Schistosoma*).

H

HAIRWORMS Common name for nematomorphs, also called "Gordian worms" or "horsehair worms" (NEMATOMORPHA).

HALTERES /**hawl**-teerz/ The highly reduced second pair of wings in flies, which do not provide lift but rather give critical assistance in keeping balance during flight (ARTHROPODA-HEXAPODA-**Insecta**-Diptera).

HAPLOID /**hap**-loyd/ **n. haploidy** /**hap**-loy-dee/ Describing cells or organisms that have a single copy of each chromosome. See also *diploid* and *polyploid*.

HAPTOCYST /**hap**-to-sist/ Type of *extrusome* on the end of suctorian *tentacles* (that is, on ends of feeding *microtubules* of a type of *sessile protist*) that discharges into prey and holds the victim to the *tentacle*; haptocysts have a complex structure and probably deliver toxins to the victim [PROTISTA-CHROMALVEOLATA-STRAMENOPILES-CILIOPHORA-INTRAMACRONUCLEATA-PHYLLOPHARYNGEA-SUCTORIA]). See also *cnidocyst*, *nematocyst* (2), and *trichocyst*.

HARVESTMAN Any member of the harmless arachnid order Opiliones (ARTHROPODA-CHELICERATA-**Arachnida**-Opiliones). Long-legged forms are called "daddy longlegs."

HEART URCHINS Common name for spatangoids, which are *irregular echinoids* that are oval, slightly flattened, and burrow in sand or mud (ECHINODERMATA-**Echinoidea-Irregularia**-Spatangoida).

HELIOZOA /**hee**-lee-o-**zo**-ah/ An obsolete *protist* group, now shown to be *polyphyletic* and with some genera yet to be reclassified; superficially resembling radiolarians ([PROTISTA-RHIZARIA-RADIOLARIA]) but with a simpler *test* and cellular structure, consisting generally of an inner *medulla* around the nucleus, an outer *cortex* with many vacuoles, and radiating *axopodia*; sometimes called "sun-animalcules."

HEMERYTHRIN /**hee**-mah-**rith**-rin/ A protein similar to *hemocyanin*, except that it uses iron to carry oxygen (ANNELIDA-**Polychaeta**-Magelonidae, BRACHIOPODA, PRIAPULIDA, SIPUNCULA). See also *hemoglobin*.

HEMIMETABOLISM /he-mee-muh-**ta-bo**-li-zuhm/ Type of development in winged insects in which the young (*nymphs*) resemble the *adults* but do not have wings and are not sexually mature (except *mayflies*, which develop complete wings at the *molt* before the final one, despite being sexually immature) (ARTHROPODA-HEXAPODA-**Insecta-Pterygota**-Blattodea, -Dermaptera, -Embiidina, -Ephemeroptera, -Hemiptera, -Isoptera, -Mantodea, -Notoptera, -Odonata, -Orthoptera, -Phasmatodea, -Phthiraptera, -Plecoptera, -Psocoptera, -Thysanoptera, -Zoraptera). Synonymous with "direct development" and "incomplete metamorphosis." See also *ametabolism* and *holometabolism*.

HEMOCOEL /**hee**-mo-seel/ In some *animals* with an *open circulatory system*, a *blood*-filled body cavity that performs many of the same functions as a *coelom* (*hydrostatic skeleton*, metabolite waste transfer); like their circulatory system and reduced *coelom*, it originates from *mesoderm*, but it does not contain the *gametes* (ARTHROPODA, CHORDATA-TUNICATA, MOLLUSCA, ONYCHOPHORA).

HEMOCYANIN /**hee**-muh-**siy**-ah-nin/ A protein used for respiration by many mollusks and arthropods that has copper at the oxygen attachment site; it is blue when oxidized (MOLLUSCA, ARTHROPODA). See also *hemerythrin* and *hemoglobin*.

HEMOGLOBIN /**hee**-muh-glo-bin/ A protein used in respiration (often called "respiratory pigments") that has iron at the oxygen-attachment site; it is red when oxidized (ANNELIDA, ARTHROPODA, MOLLUSCA). See also *hemerythrin*, *hemocyanin*, and *myoglobin*.

HEMOLYMPH /**hee**-mo-limf/ Specialized term for the *blood* of an *animal* with an *open circulatory system* (especially ARTHROPODA, MOLLUSCA).

HEPATIC CECUM /hee-**pa**-tik **see**-kuhm/ See *pyloric cecum*.

HERMAPHRODITIC /huhr-**maf**-ro-**di**-tik/ Having both sexes in one individual; from Hermaphroditus of Greek mythology, the androgynous offspring of the deities Hermes and Aphrodite. See also *monoecious*.

HERMATYPIC /**huhr**-mah-**ti**-pik/ Type of *coral* that builds *reefs* (CNIDARIA-**Anthozoa** especially -**Hexacorallia**-Scleractinia).

HETEROTROPHIC /he-tuhr-o-**tro**-fik/ Requiring the consumption of other organisms as a source of carbon.

HETEROZOOID /he-tuhr-o-**zo**-id/ One of two main types of ectoproct *zooid*, usually responsible for cleaning the colony of debris; there are two types of heterozooids, *avicularia* and *vibracula*; the other main type of ectoproct *zooid* is the *autozoid*, a feeding *polyp* (ECTOPROCTA).

HEXACANTH /**heks**-uh-kanth/ The first *larval* stage of *tapeworms*, which is derived from *micromeres*, has six hooks, and is encased in two *embryonic envelopes*; the hexacanth and its envelopes are together called an *oncosphere* and will develop further into either a *cysticercus* or *procercoid larva*. (PLATYHELMINTHES-**Cestoda**).

HINDGUT Used mostly for arthropods, this is the posterior end of the *alimentary canal*, specialized for the absorption of water and formation of *feces*. The hindgut and the *foregut* are *ectodermally* derived and lined with *cuticle* (ARTHROPODA). See also *midgut*.

HOLDFAST Any structure that affixes an organism to the substrate, most commonly used for *stalked jellyfish* and the adhesive and/or gripping *stalk* ends of crinoids (CNIDARIA-**Staurozoa**, ECHINODERMATA-**Crinoidea**).

HOLOBLASTIC CLEAVAGE /ho-lo-**blas**-tik/ In early *embryology*, this is a type of *cleavage* in which the divisions completely separate the *cytoplasm* of the *egg*.

HOLOMETABOLISM /ho-lo-me-**ta**-bo-li-zuhm/ Type of development in winged insects consisting of three distinct stages: *larva, pupa*, and *adult* (ARTHROPODA-HEXAPODA-**Insecta**-**Pterygota**-Coleoptera, -Diptera, -Hymenoptera, -Lepidoptera, -Mecoptera, -Megaloptera, -Neuroptera, -Raphidioptera, -Siphonaptera, -Strepsiptera, -Trichoptera). Synonymous with "indirect development" and "complete metamorphosis." See also *ametabolism* and *hemimetabolism*.

HOMOLOGOUS /ho-**mah**-lo-guhs/ Describing features (structures or behavior) that are similar due to shared ancestry; often used to describe the two versions of the functionally identical chromosomes inherited by a *diploid* organism from its parents. See also *analogous*.

HOMOTHETOGENIC FISSION /ho-mo-**thee**-to-**je**-nik …/ Type of *binary fission* in *ciliated protists* that cuts across the *kinety system* and creates daughter cells that are not reflected duplicates of each other ([PROTISTA-CHROMALVEOLATA-STRAMENOPILES-CILIOPHORA]). See also *symmetrogenic fission*.

HORSEHAIR WORMS Common name for nematomorphs, also called "Gordian worms" or just "hairworms" (NEMATOMORPHA).

HORSESHOE CRABS Common name for large marine chelicerates currently found in East and Southeast Asia, as well as along the East coast of North and Central America (ARTHROPODA-CHELICERATA-**Merostomata**-Xiphosura).

HYALINE CAP /**hiy**-ah-leen …/ The clear portion of *ectoplasm* at the tip of *protist pseudopods* where *endoplasm* becomes *ectoplasm* ([PROTISTA especially -AMOEBOZOA]).

HYDATID /hiy-**dah**-tid/ Name for a large *cyst* that contains one or more *tapeworm cysticerci larvae*; this term is most commonly used when *cysticerci* enter the wrong *intermediate host* and the resulting *cysts* cause significant damage to whatever organs they invade (most commonly the liver, brain, lungs, spleen, kidneys, or bones) (PLATYHELMINTHES-**Cestoda**).

HYDRANTH /**hiy**-dranth/ The part of a *gastrozooid* where the *mouth* and *tentacles* are located (CNIDARIA-**Hydrozoa**).

HYDROCAULUS /**hiy**-dro-**caw**-luhs/ In colonial hydrozoans, the *stalk* of the colony that connects individual *zooids*, composed of *coenosarc* and *perisarc* (CNIDARIA-**Hydrozoa**).

HYDROCOEL /**hiy**-dro-seel/ In *embryonic* echinoderms, the *coelomic* pocket that forms between the *axocoel* and the *somatocoel* (ECHINODERMATA).

HYDROGENOSOME /**hiy**-dro-**je**-no-som/ A mitochondrion-derived *organelle* found in some *protists*, *animals*, and fungi that generates ATP from pyruvate (an energy-storing molecule derived from glucose via pyruvic acid); byproducts include CO_2 and H_2; it is used in *anoxic* conditions (especially [PROTISTA-EXCAVATA-PARABASALIA, -CHROMALVEOLATA-STRAMENOPILES-CILIOPHORA]).

HYDROID /**hiy**-droyd/ Common term often used to refer to a hydrozoan (CNIDARIA-**Hydrozoa**), derived from the obsolete taxonomic class "Hydroida."

HYDROSTATIC SKELETON /**hiy**-dro-**sta**-tik …/ The *coelomic* fluid (or *hemocoel* fluid) when used under pressure as support for the body shape and muscular contraction.

HYDROTHECA /**hiy**-dro-**thee**-ka/ In colonial hydrozoans, the *perisarc* at the base of the *hydranth* where it expands into a wide cup (CNIDARIA-**Hydrozoa**).

HYPOBRANCHIAL GLANDS /**hiy**-po-**bran**-kee-ahl …/ *Glands* in the *mantle cavities* of mollusks that secrete mucous (MOLLUSCA-**Gastropoda**).

HYPODERMIC IMPREGNATION Type of fertilization in some *flatworms* in which one worm penetrates the body wall of another worm with a needle-like *penis* to inject *sperm* (PLATYHELMINTHES-**Turbellaria**). See also *bursa copulatrix* and *love dart*.

HYPODERMIS Alternative name for the *epidermis* of arthropods, since it lies under the *exoskeleton* (ARTHROPODA).

HYPOSTOME /**hiy**-po-stome/ The circular area of a cnidarian *polyp* that is between the *tentacles* and the *mouth* (CNIDARIA).

I, J, K, L

IMAGO /i-**may**-go/ **pl. imagoes or imagines** /i-**may**-guh-neez/ The *adult* stage of an insect (ARTHROPODA-HEXAPODA-**Insecta**). See also *subimago*.

INCOMPLETE GUT An *alimentary canal* that has a *mouth* but no *anus*; undigested material is *egested* out of the *mouth*; inapplicable where the *gut* is missing entirely (CNIDARIA, BRACHIOPODA-**Articulata**, CTENOPHORA [but see also *anal pore*], ECHINODERMATA-**Ophiuroidea**, GNATHOSTOMULIDA, MICROGNATHOZOA [usually], PLATYHELMINTHES, ROTIFERA [sometimes], [XENACOELOMORPHA]). See also *complete gut*.

INCOMPLETE METAMORPHOSIS See *hemimetabolism*.

INCURRENT SIPHON or INCURRENT CANAL /in-kur-rent …/ A channel through which water enters a *syconoid* or *leuconoid sponge* (PORIFERA). For tunicates see *buccal siphon/canal*, and for mollusks see *inhalant siphon/canal*.

INDETERMINATE DEVELOPMENT Type of development in which cell differentiation is not determined from the first division of the *zygote*, and separated *blastomeres* can fully develop (DEUTEROSTOMIA). See also *determinate development* and *radial cleavage*.

INDIRECT DEVELOPMENT See *holometabolism*.

INFUSORIFORM LARVA /in-fyoo-**so**-ree-form …/ *Larva* of the dicyemids that results from the union of *egg* and *sperm* produced by the *axial cell* (DICYEMIDA).

INGRESSION /in-**gre**-shuhn/ Type of *gastrulation* in which some cells of the *blastula* detach and migrate into the *blastocoel* where they proliferate, eventually forming the *endoderm*. In "unipolar" ingression, cells migrate from only one pole; in "multipolar" ingression, cells migrate inward from both poles.

INHALANT SIPHON or INHALANT CANAL /in-**hay**-luhnt …/ The roll of tissue through which water enters the *mantle cavity* of bivalves and gastropods (MOLLUSCA-**Bivalvia**, -**Gastropoda**). For tunicates see *buccal siphon/canal*, and for *sponges* see *incurrent siphon/canal*.

INK SAC A complex *diverticulum* of the *rectum* of cephalopods where ink (a solution of melanin) is secreted and stored to be used as a screen during escape (MOLLUSCA-**Cephalopoda**).

INSTAR /**in**-stahr/ Any stage between two *molts* of an insect; insect *larvae* are commonly described by their current instar number, such a "first instar" for a hatchling, "second instar" after one *molt*, etc. (ARTHROPODA-HEXAPODA-**Insecta**).

INTERMEDIATE HOST Any host where a *parasite* lives but does not reproduce sexually. See also *definitive host*.

INTERRADIAL CANALS /in-tuhr-**ray**-dee-uhl …/ In scyphozoan *medusae*, those *radial canals* that form a branching network connecting the outer margins of the *gastric pouches* to the *ring canal* (CNIDARIA-**Scyphozoa**). Occasionally and erroneously used for any branching *radial canals*, including *perradial canals*, or, in the English translation of Beklemishev's *Principles of Comparative Anatomy of Invertebrates* (1969, vol. 1, p. 43), erroneously used to refer to the unbranched *radial canals*. See also *adradial canals* and *perradial canals*.

INTERTENTACULAR ORGAN /**in**-tuhr-ten-**tak**-yoo-lahr .../ Specialized tube in between two *tentacles* of ectoprocts through which the *oocyte* leaves the *autozooid* (ECTOPROCTA).

INTESTINE /in-**tes**-tin/ General term for the section of the *alimentary canal* between the *stomach* and the *anus*.

INTRACAPSULAR CYTOPLASM /in-trah-**kap**-soo-luhr **siy**-to-**pla**-zuhm/ See *endoplasm* (2).

INVAGINATION /in-**va**-ji-**nay**-shuhn/ A mode of *gastrulation* in which certain cells of the *blastula* multiply more rapidly than other cells, forming a blind sac into the *blastula* which extends and becomes the *archenteron*.

INVOLUTION /**in**-vo-**loo**-shuhn/ A type of *gastrulation* somewhat like *invagination* in that certain cells of the *blastula* proliferate and make an inpocketing, but in this case the inward migrating cells form a sheet that grows in close contact with the outer cells, ultimately proliferating around the entire inside of the *blastula* and forming *endoderm*.

IRREGULAR ECHINOIDS /... e-ki-noydz/ Echinoids in the aptly named infraclass Irregularia, which are more *bilaterally symmetrical* than other echinoids, and which have both the *mouth* and *anus* on the *oral* surface; they commonly burrow in the mud and sand (ECHINODERMATA-**Echinoidea-Irregularia**).

ISOGAMOUS /**iy**-so-**ga**-muhs/ The uncommon condition of having morphologically similar *gametes*, thus rendering the terms "male" and "female" meaningless in these taxa ([PROTISTA]).

JAW Although vague, this usually refers to any hinged or pinching structure at the beginning of the *alimentary canal*. See also *mandible*.

JAW WORMS Common name for the gnathostomulids, a phylum of microscopic marine worms (GNATHOSTOMULIDA).

JELLYFISH Common name for a *medusa* (CNIDARIA-**Cubozoa**, -**Hydrozoa**, -**Scyphozoa**, -**Staurozoa**). See also *box jellyfish*.

JUVENILE General term for any sexually immature individual past the early *embryonic* stages.

KENOZOOID /**ke**-nuh-**zo**-id/ Type of ectoproct *zooid* that forms supporting structures, such as *stalks* and *stolons* (ECTOPROCTA).

KIDNEY Generally used to refer to any *excretory* organ, but see *nephridium*.

KINETOPLAST /ki-**ne**-to-plast/ The DNA-containing portion of an enlarged mitochondrion in one group of *protists*, the "kinetoplastids" ([PROTISTA-EXCAVATA-EUGLENOZOA-KINETOPLASTEA]).

KINETOSOME /ki-**ne**-to-some/ See *basal body*.

KINETY SYSTEM /ki-**ne**-tee …/ In *protists* the complex nerve-like control system formed by connecting the *basal bodies* of numerous *flagella* and *cilia* ([PROTISTA]).

KRILL /kril/ *Pelagic*, marine crustaceans in the order Euphausiacea (ARTHROPODA-CRUSTACEA-**Malacostraca**-Euphausiacea).

LABIAL PALPS /**lay**-bee-ahl …/ 1. Two fleshy projections on either side of bivalve *mouths* where food from the *ctenidia* is sorted before entering the *mouth* (MOLLUSCA-**Bivalvia**). 2. The jointed extensions of the second *maxillae* (*labium*) of insects, used as sensory structures (ARTHROPODA-HEXAPODA-**Insecta**).

LABIUM /**lay**-bee-uhm/ 1. Any lip-like structure. 2. In arthropods (especially insects and crustaceans), the structure posterior to the mouth formed by the fused bases of the second *maxillae*; like most arthropod mouthparts it may be highly modified (ARTHROPODA especially -CRUSTACEA, -HEXAPODA, also -MYRIAPODA).

LABRUM /**lay**-bruhm/ The "upper lip" of arthropods (especially myriapods, insects, and crustaceans); it is a hinged extension of the *clypeus* (ARTHROPODA especially -CRUSTACEA, -HEXAPODA, -MYRIAPODA).

LANCELET /**lan**-suh-let/ A member of the chordate subphylum Cephalochordata (CHORDATA-CEPHALOCHORDATA). See also *amphioxus*.

LARVA /**lahr**-vah/ A *juvenile* or *embryonic* stage that usually has few morphological or ecological similarities with the *adult*.

LATERAL LOBES In trilobites, the two lobes extending along the sides of the body (ARTHROPODA-TRILOBITA). See also *axial lobe*.

LECITHAL /**le**-si-thahl/**or LECITHIC** /**les**-i-thik/ Containing *yolk*.

LECITHOTROPHIC /luh-**si**-tho-**tro**-pik/ Relying on *yolk* for nutrition.

LEECHES Common name for hirudinids (ANNELIDA-**Hirudinea**).

LEGS Although it may seem odd to define such a common word, odder still is the fact that it often gets clarified as "walking legs" in scientific writings on invertebrates (a phrase for which one can also get a scolding from an editor). The word "leg" refers not only to any *appendage* used for walking, but also to an *appendage* used for walking in most of the animal's closest relatives, regardless of how it is modified in the lineage of interest. For example, in arachnids, which lack *antennae*, some groups have had one of their pairs of walking *appendages* (legs) evolve into structures that today are elongate, sensory, and unable to bear weight, and these are still referred to as legs. See also *ovigerous legs*.

LEISHMANIASIS Widespread disease of varying severity caused by a genus of *kinetoplastids* ([PROTISTA-EXCAVATA-EUGLENOZOA-KINETOPLASTEA-METAKINETOPLASTINA]-*Leishmania*); it is spread by sand flies (ARTHROPODA-HEXAPODA-**Insecta**-Diptera-Psychodidae-Phlebotiminae).

LEUCONOID /**loo**-kah-noyd/ The most complex body plan of *sponges*, consisting mainly of many small *flagellated chambers* throughout the entire body, which are connected by canals that eventually lead to an *excurrent canal* and *osculum*; the *spicules* are usually siliceous (PORIFERA). See also *asconoid* and *syconoid*.

LIGULA /**lig**-yoo-lah/ 1. The terminal lobe of an insect *labium* (ARTHROPODA-HEXAPODA-**Insecta**). 2. The flattened lobe that constitutes the main portion of the polychaete *neuropodium* or *notopodium* (ANNELIDA-**Polychaeta**).

LIMPETS /**lim**-pets/ Common name for gastropods that have a shallow, conical shell; "keyhole limpets" have a hole at the point of the shell (MOLLUSCA-**Gastropoda** especially -[PATELLOGASTROPODA]).

LITTORAL /**li**-tuh-rahl/ Any aquatic region (freshwater or marine) shallow enough to have rooted plants and penetration of light to the bottom.

LIVER Although this word almost always refers to the multifaceted organ in vertebrates, it is sometimes used for the molluscan digestive *diverticula* (MOLLUSCA). Synonymous with "digestive gland" in mollusks.

LOBOPODIUM /lo-bo-**po**-dee-uhm/ A broad, unsupported type of *pseudopodium* formed out of *endoplasm* and *ectoplasm*, exemplified by amoebas ([PROTISTA especially -AMOEBOZOA]).

LOPHOPHORATES /lo-fo-**for**-ayts/ Those phyla that have a *lophophore*. Previously this included the phylum Entoprocta, which is now considered to be most closely related to the phylum Cycliophora (tiny *animals* that live on crustacean mouthparts). The ring of *tentacles* in entoprocts does not fit the definition of a lophophore in that the *tentacles* are not hollow and appear to be formed from the body wall; cycliophorans lack *tentacles* altogether, and instead each has a ring of "compound *cilia*" (bundles of joined *cilia*) around its *mouth*. All five phyla are within the *protostome* clade *Spiralia* (those invertebrates that do not *molt*), and the ectoprocts are often considered sister to the entoprocts plus cycliophorans; nonetheless, the relationship among these phyla and the nature and taxonomic importance of the lophophore are still under study (BRACHIOPODA, ECTOPROCTA, PHORONIDA, previously ENTOPROCTA, in some texts CYCLIOPHORA).

LOPHOPHORE /**lo**-fo-for/ The set of *ciliated*, *coelom*-filled *tentacles* arranged in whorls, arcs, or a ring around the mouth in three phyla, used for capturing food and reproduction (BRACHIOPODA, ECTOPROCTA, PHORONIDA).

LOPHOTROCHOZOA /lo-fo-**tro**-ko-**zo**-ah/ See *Spiralia.*

LORICA /**lor**-i-kah/ 1. In euglenids, choanoflagellates, and some ciliates, a loose, protective covering that is often proteinaceous and inflexible; in choanoflagellates it may have supporting siliceous rods; (*protist* coverings that fit tightly on or are in the cell are called *shells* or *tests*) ([PROTISTA-CHROMALVEOLATA-STRAMENOPILES-CILIOPHORA, -EXCAVATA-EUGLENOZOA, -OPISTHOKONTA-CHOANOMONADA]). 2. The thickened *cuticle* of rotifers into which the body can withdraw (ROTIFERA). 3. A loriciferan structure *analogous* in origin and function to the rotifer lorica (LORICIFERA). 4. The *abdominal* covering of priapulid *larvae* that consists of several plates and is regularly *molted* (PRIAPULIDA).

LOVE DART A sharp, *calcareous* structure forcibly inserted into a mating partner in certain land *snails*; the dart is covered in mucous and *gland* products, which enter the recipient's *hemolymph*, and some love darts are hollow and function like the needle of a syringe; the love dart is received by the *sperm* recipient (these *animals* are *hermaphroditic*) and promotes *sperm* storage instead of their digestion; the organ holding the dart, associated *glands*, and the injection apparatus is the *dart sac* (MOLLUSCA-**Gastropoda**-[PULMONATA]). See also *bursa copulatrix* and *hypodermic impregnation*.

LUMEN /loo-men/ An uncommon term for the space inside an *alimentary canal*, *blood* vessel, or other tubular structure; sometimes also used for the inside of any hollow organ or even the interiors of subcellular structures. See also *atrium*, *antrum*, *bursa*, *cecum*, *diverticulum*, and *sinus*. Lumen is a term that demonstrates the slight differences of meaning among these words, such as whether they are used for the *alimentary canal*, any elongate organ, or any hollow organ. Another distinction is whether they refer to just the space inside a structure or also to the structure that makes the space, a difference that may depend on whether the structure has more descriptive purposes than to make the space, such as digestion or circulation.

M

MACROGAMETE /**mak**-ro-**ga**-meet/ See *egg*; see also *gamont*.

MACROGAMETOCYTE /**mak**-ro-ga-**meet**-o-siyt/ See *gamont*.

MACROGAMONT /**mak**-ro-**ga**-mawnt/ See *gamont*.

MACROMERES /**mak**-ro-meerz/ *Blastomeres* that are large and usually filled with *yolk*. See also *micromeres* and *vegetal pole*.

MACRONUCLEUS /**mak**-ro-**noo**-klee-uhs/ The *polyploid* nucleus of ciliates; it is used for mitosis and protein synthesis ([PROTISTA-CHROMALVEOLATA-STRAMENOPILES-CILIOPHORA]).

MACROSCLERE /**mak**-ro-skleer/ A large type of *spicule* (PORIFERA).

MADREPORITE /**mad**-ruh-**por**-iyt/ In echinoderms, the small, round plate that separates the *water-vascular system* from the environment. It is a sieve-like, hard plate that marks the beginning of the *stone canal*; in *sea cucumbers* it leads to the *coelom* instead of the outside (ECHINODERMATA).

MAGGOTS /**ma**-guhts/ Common term for certain fly *larvae* that lack legs and live inside their food source (ARTHROPODA-HEXAPODA-**Insecta**-Diptera-Brachycera).

MALARIA A worldwide and often deadly disease of
humans and other vertebrates caused by certain species
of *protist* that enter red *blood* cells and then invade the *liver*
and (in some cases) the brain ([PROTISTA-
CHROMALVEOLATA-STRAMENOPILES-
APICOMPLEXA-ACONOIDASIDA-
HAEMOSPORORIDA]-*Plasmodium*); it is spread by
mosquitoes in the genus *Anopheles* (ARTHROPODA-
HEXAPODA-**Insecta**-<u>Diptera</u>-Culicidae).

MALPIGHIAN TUBULES /mal-**pi**-gi-ahn …/ The thread-
like tubes that extend from the juncture between the *midgut*
and *hindgut* of insects, myriapods, arachnids, and tardigrades;
they are used in *excretion*, collecting *nitrogenous wastes* from the
hemocoel and secreting them into the *alimentary canal*
(ARTHROPODA-CHELICERATA-**Arachnida**,
-HEXAPODA, -MYRIAPODA, TARDIGRADA).

MANDIBLE /**man**-di-buhl/ Generally, a structure (usually
paired *appendages* in invertebrates, but not so in vertebrates)
near or in the *mouth* that can hold and crush food before it
is fully ingested; essentially, part of a *jaw*. It is most
commonly used to refer to the primary mouthparts of
crustaceans, insects, and myriapods. In crustaceans,
mandibles are the third paired head *appendages*; in insects
and myriapods they are directly posterior to the *labrum*
(especially ARTHROPODA-CRUSTACEA,
-HEXAPODA, -MYRIAPODA).

MANTLE 1. The outer layer of tissue that encloses most (if
not all) of the body in mollusks and brachiopods, and
which usually secretes the *shell* (BRACHIOPODA,
MOLLUSCA). 2. In *barnacles*, the enveloping tissue that
forms the cavity into which the animal withdraws its
appendages, sometimes called the *carapace*

(ARTHROPODA-CRUSTACEA-**Maxillopoda-Cirripedia**).

MANTLE CAVITY 1. In mollusks, the *invagination* under the *mantle* that contains the *gills*, *osphradium*, *anus*, and *gonopores* (MOLLUSCA). 2. In brachiopods, a cavity *analogous* to that in mollusks, just inside the two *valves* and filled mostly by the *lophophore* (BRACHIOPODA). 3. In *barnacles*, the protected cavity that holds most of the *animal's* organs and *appendages* (ARTHROPODA-CRUSTACEA-**Maxillopoda**-**Cirripedia**).

MANUBRIUM /muh-**noo**-bri-uhm/ 1. The extensions of tissue around the *mouths* of non-scyphozoan *medusae*, possibly *homologous* to the *hypostome* of *polyps* and the *oral arms* of scyphozoan *medusae* (CNIDARIA-**Cubozoa**, -**Hydrozoa**, -**Staurozoa**). 2. In collembola, the fused bases of the paired *appendages* on the fourth *abdominal segment* used for jumping (*furca*) (ARTHROPODA-HEXAPODA-**Entognatha**-**Collembola**).

MASTAX /**mas**-taks/ The hard, muscular *pharynx* of rotifers (ROTIFERA).

MAXILLAE /mak-**sil**-lee/ **sing. maxilla** /mak-**sil**-luh/ In many arthropods (especially crustaceans, insects, and myriapods), the paired head *appendages* that are posterior to the *mandibles*; there are often two pairs of *maxillae*, the second pair of which may be fused to form the *labium* (ARTHROPODA especially -CRUSTACEA, -HEXAPODA, -MYRIAPODA).

MAXILLIPED /mak-**si**-li-ped/ In crustaceans, an anterior *thoracopod* used alongside head appendages, usually for processing food (ARTHROPODA-CRUSTACEA). See also *maxillae* and *pereiopod*.

MAYFLIES Common name for an order of insects with aquatic *larvae* and a highly synchronized, mass emergence of winged stages (ARTHROPODA-HEXAPODA-**Insecta**-Ephemeroptera).

MECHANOSENSORY, MECHANORECEPTOR, and MECHANORECEPTION The ability to detect, organ for detecting, and act of detecting (respectively) changes in movement, pressure, or other forces, such as gravity.

MEDULLA /mah-**doo**-lah/ In *heliozoans*, the inner region of *cytoplasm* that contains the nucleus. (In the similar-looking radiolarians—[PROTISTA-RHIZARIA-RADIOLARIA]—the inner capsule of the *test* [or inner capsules, for there can be more than one] is referred to as the "medullary shell[s].")

MEDUSA /me-**doo**-sah/ The cnidarian body form that is usually free-swimming (attached in the Staurozoa) and sexual, commonly called a "jellyfish" (CNIDARIA-**Cubozoa**, -**Hydrozoa**, -**Scyphozoa**, -**Staurozoa**). See also *polyp*.

MEGALOPS / MEGALOPA /**me**-gah-lahps / me-gah-**lah**-pah/ In brachyuran *crabs*, the *larval* stage following the *zoea* (ARTHROPODA-CRUSTACEA-**Malacostraca**-Decapoda-Brachyura). Synonymous with "postlarva." See also *nauplius*.

MEHLIS' GLAND /**may**-lis …/ In *flukes*, the large, single-celled *gland* that surrounds the *ootype* and probably begins the formation of the *egg shell* (PLATYHELMINTHES-**Trematoda**); often written without the apostrophe and not seen with an "s" after the apostrophe. Synonymous with "shell gland."

MEMBRANELLE /mem-brah-**nel**/ In ciliates, a structure composed of several *cilia* arranged in a compact row; membranelles usually occur in groups or rows ([PROTISTA-CHROMALVEOLATA-STRAMENOPILES-CILIOPHORA]). See also *ctene* and *undulating membrane*.

MEROBLASTIC CLEAVAGE /**mer**-uh-**blas**-tik/ Type of *embryonic cleavage* in which the separations between the new cells are not complete.

MEROGONY /mer-**aw**-je-nee/ See *schizogony*.

MEROZOITE /mer-o-**zo**-iyt/ In apicomplexans, a type of offspring produced by a *schizont* (a stage that reproduces asexually via the preliminary division of the nucleus several times); the merozoite has one nucleus and is released into the bloodstream where it enters *blood* cells and becomes a *trophozoite* ([PROTISTA-CHROMALVEOLATA-STRAMENOPILES-APICOMPLEXA]).

MESENTERIC FILAMENT /me-sen-**teyr**-ik …/ In *sea anemones*, the cord of tissue that runs along the edge of an incomplete *mesentery* and which bears *glandular* cells and *cnidocytes*; it is used in digestion and becomes an *acontium* toward the *pedal disc* (CNIDARIA-**Anthozoa**). Synonymous with "gastric filament" and "septal filament."

MESENTERY /me-sen-teyr-ee/ 1. A vertical sheet of tissue that divides the *gastrovascular cavity* of *sea anemones*. *Sea anemones* have several mesenteries, and they can be "complete" (connecting the *actinopharynx* with the body column, also called "primary") or "incomplete" (having one side connected to the inside of the body column and the other side edged with a *mesenteric filament*, also called "secondary" and "tertiary") (CNIDARIA-**Anthozoa**).

2. Generally any sheet of tissue that envelops, separates, or supports particular organs or body regions.

MESENTOBLAST /me-**zen**-to-blast/ Name for the 4D cell in *spiralian embryos* that eventually gives rise to *mesoderm* and sometimes also *endoderm* (thus the name); especially applicable to annelids, which were among the first models in embryology; in annelids the mesentoblast first produces *teloblasts*; (The 4D cell is so named because it is a fourth derivative in the "D quadrant" [also called the "dorsal quadrant"]) (especially ANNELIDA).

MESODERM /me-zuh-derm/ The middle layer of cells in an early *embryo* that develops into the muscle, *blood* vessels, and various organs.

MESOGLEA /me-zuh-glee-ah/ In cnidarians, the layer of jelly-like substance between the *epidermis* and *gastrodermis*; it is especially thick in the *jellyfish* of scyphozoans, and it contains some cells (CNIDARIA). See also *diploblastic*.

MESOHYL /me-zo-hiyl/ In *sponges*, the cellular and proteinaceous layer between the outer covering of cells (*pinacoderm*) and the inner lining of *collar cells*; it contains fibers of *spongin* or *collagen*, spicules (if present), and *amoebocytes* (PORIFERA).

MESOZOA /me-so-**zo**-ah/ Former phylum that contained the orthonectids and dicyemids (also called "Rhombozoa"), both of which are tiny, *parasitic*, marine *animals*, as well as the dubious monoblastozoans and the tiny, sheet-like placozoans. Each of these four taxa has been moved into its own phylum, and their relationships to each other and other phyla are still being studied; Monoblastozoa has not been seen since its discovery in 1892 (DICYEMIDA, MONOBLASTOZOA, ORTHONECTIDA, PLACOZOA).

METACERCARIA /me-tah-ser-**keyr**-ee-ah/ The *encysted cercaria* after it has entered the tissues of the *intermediate host* (PLATYHELMINTHES-**Trematoda**).

METAMERE /**me**-tah-meer/ A *segment* that extends to the internal organs and *coelom*, such as in the annelids; often called a "true *segment*" (ANNELIDA). See also *annulus* (2), *somite*, *tagma*, and *telson*.

METAMORPHOSIS /me-tah-**mor**-fo-sis/ A transition from one developmental stage to another that is characterized by significant physiological and morphological changes.

METANEPHRIDIUM /me-tah-ne-**frid**-ee-uhm/ A *nephridium* that uses a *ciliated*, *funnel*-shaped structure inside the *coelom* to collect fluids, which are then moved to the outside of the body via a distinct tube that is not merged with a *coelomoduct*. See also *protonephridium* and *mixonephridium*.

METASOMA /me-tah-**so**-mah/ See *postabdomen*.

METATROCH /**me**-tah-trahk/ One of two *ciliated* bands around the middle of a *trochophore larva*, this one located on the same side as the *anus*. See also *prototroch*.

METAZOAN /me-tah-**zo**-ahn/ See *animal*.

METECDYSIS /met-ek-**diy**-sis/ Stage of arthropod *molting* during which the new *cuticle* is hardened and the *animal* recovers its ability to move; it continues to swell its body while the new *cuticle* is still flexible, and in crustaceans calcium is moved from the *gastroliths* to the *exoskeleton* (ARTHROPODA). Also called "postecdysis" and "postmolt." See also *anecdysis*, *ecdysis*, and *proecdysis*.

MICROFILAMENTS Long polymers of the protein "actin" that form intracellular supports and locomotory mechanisms. See also *microtubule*.

MICROGAMETE /**miy**-kro-**ga**-meet/ See *sperm*; see also *gamont*.

MICROGAMETOCYTE /**miy**-kro-ga-**mee**-to-siyt/ See *gamont*.

MICROGAMONT /**miy**-kro-**ga**-mawnt/ See *gamont*.

MICROMERES /**miy**-kro-meerz/ Small *blastomeres* which lack *yolk*. See also *animal pole* and *macromeres*.

MICRONUCLEUS /**miy**-kro-**noo**-klee-uhs/ In ciliates, the smaller of two types of nuclei; it is responsible for reproduction, undergoing meiosis, and producing the new *macronuclei* during *conjugation* ([PROTISTA-CHROMALVEOLATA-STRAMENOPILES-CILIOPHORA]). See also *macronucleus*.

MICROPYLE /**miy**-kro-**piyl**/ The place on a *sponge gemmule* that will be the exit for the internal *embryo* (PORIFERA-**Demospongiae**-Spongillidae).

MICROSCLERE /**miy**-kro-skleer/ A small type of *sponge spicule* (PORIFERA).

MICROTUBULE /**miy**-kro-**too**-byool/ A tiny tube composed of the protein "tubulin," used in cells for locomotion, reproduction, and support; microtubules make up *cilia*, *flagella*, spindle fibers, and supporting structures in the *cytoplasm*.

MICROVILLI /**miy**-kro-**vil**-lee/ **sing. microvillus** /miy-kro-**vil**-us/ Tiny, thin extensions of a cell surface.

MIDGUT The section of the arthropod *alimentary canal* between the *foregut* and *hindgut*; it is derived from *endoderm* and is specialized for enzyme secretion and nutrient absorption (ARTHROPODA).

MIRACIDIUM /mir-ah-**sid**-ee-uhm/ In *digenetic flukes*, the *ciliated larval* stage that hatches from the *egg* and infects the *intermediate host*, either through penetration of the skin or ingestion of the *egg* (PLATYHELMINTHES-**Trematoda**).

MIXONEPHRIDIUM /**mik**-so-ne-**frid**-ee-uhm/ A structure that results from the complete union of a *metanephridium* and a *coelomoduct*, such that a single tube with a ciliated *funnel* inside the *coelomic* cavity can carry fluid, *nitrogenous wastes*, *gametes*, and other items to the outside. (Partial mergings of *nephridia* and *coelomoducts* are called "protonephromixia" and "metanephromixia.") See also *protonephridium*.

MOLT 1. To undergo the hormonally-controlled process of shedding one *cuticle* (or *exoskeleton*) in order to allow growth of the organism and the subsequent replacement of the *cuticle*. See also *ecdysis*. 2. A specific life stage between two molting events (e.g., "the first molt"). See also *instar*. 3. The *cuticle* or *exoskeleton* that was shed during *molting*.

MONOECIOUS /**maw**-no-**ee**-shuhs/ Describing species in which both male and female organs and *gametes* are produced by single individuals. Synonymous with "hermaphroditic." See also *dioecious*.

MONOGENETIC /**maw**-no-je-**ne**-tik/ Referring to *flukes* that have only one host (PLATYHELMINTHES-**Monogenea**).

MONOPHYLETIC /**maw**-no-fiy-**le**-tik/ Describing a group of taxa whose members all descend from a common ancestor and includes all of that ancestor's descendants.

MOTHER-OF-PEARL See *nacre*. Sometimes written without dashes.

MOUTH The opening to the *alimentary canal* where food enters (not found in [ACANTHOCEPHALA], ANNELIDA-**Polychaeta**-Canalipalpata-Siboglinidae [deep-sea worms that include the former phyla Pogonophora and Vestimentifera], PLATYHELMINTHES-**Cestoda**, and NEMATOMORPHA).

MULTIPLE FISSION See *schizogony*.

MUTUALISM /**myoo**-choo-wahl-izm/ A relationship between two species in which both benefit from the other's presence. See also *symbiosis*.

MYOCYTES /**miy**-o-siyts/ Contractile cells found in the *mesohyl* of some *sponges*; they are especially useful in regulating the size of the *osculum* (PORIFERA).

MYOEPITHELIUM /**miy**-o-ep-e-**thee**-lee-uhm/ Tissue composed of *epithelial* cells that can also contract somewhat, like muscle cells (especially CNIDARIA).

MYOGLOBIN /**miy**-o-glo-bin/ A protein that has a higher affinity for oxygen than *hemoglobin* and is thus used for oxygen storage in muscles.

MYONEME /**miy**-o-neem/ The *protist* equivalent of a muscle fiber, this is a contractile fiber inside the *pellicle* of mainly *sessile* forms ([PROTISTA]).

MYXOPODIUM /mik-so-**po**-dee-uhm/ See *reticulopodium*.

MYXOZOA /mik-so-**zo**-ah/ A large group of *parasitic* cnidarians that are so reduced anatomically, they were originally classified as protists; their *definitive host* is an invertebrate, such as an annelid, and their *intermediate host* is usually a fish (CNIDARIA-[MYXOZOA]).

N, O

NACRE /**nay**-kur/ The layer of inorganic material deposited by the *mantle* that lines the inside of the molluscan *shell*, as well as foreign deposits caught between the *mantle* and the *shell* (which can become pearls); it is often iridescent and is composed of calcium carbonate crystals arranged in layers held together by various organic compounds (including *chitin*) (MOLLUSCA). Synonymous with "mother-of-pearl" and "nacreous layer."

NACREOUS LAYER /**nay**-kree-uhs …/ See *nacre*.

NAIAD /**nay**-ad, **nay**-uhd, or **niy**-ad/ The aquatic *larva* of a *hemimetabolous* insect (that is, an aquatic *nymph*) (ARTHROPODA-HEXAPODA-**Insecta**-Ephemeroptera, -Odonata, -Plecoptera).

NAUPLIUS /**naw**-plee-uhs/ The first *larval* stage of crustaceans; it usually hatches from the *egg* but is sometimes completed before hatching; it has two pairs of *antennae*, a pair of *mandibles*, and a medial *eye*; it develops into other *larval* forms, at which time it develops its other *appendages*; crustacean larvae are diverse in morphology, alternative names, and stages before adulthood, and the three defined in this glossary (*nauplius*, *zoea*, and *megalops*) are simply the most well-known and easiest for a beginner to learn (ARTHROPODA-CRUSTACEA).

NECTOPHORE /**nek**-tuh-for/ In some free-floating or free-swimming hydrozoan colonies, the highly modified *medusa* that remains with the colony and pulsates for colony locomotion (CNIDARIA-**Hydrozoa**-Siphonophorae).

NEEDHAM'S SAC /**nee**-duhms .../ See *spermatophoric sac*.

NEMATOCYST /nee-**ma**-to-sist/ 1. The most common type of *cnidocyst*, characterized by having a thread with barbs and, in the undischarged state, both helical and lengthwise (accordion-like) pleats that shorten its length considerably (CNIDARIA). See also *ptychocyst* and *spirocyst*. 2. An *organelle* in some dinoflagellates that consists of an eversible thread, much like a *cnidocyst* in cnidarians or *haptocyst* in ciliates ([PROTISTA-CHROMALVEOLATA-ALVEOLATA-DINOZOA-DINOFLAGELLATA]).

NEMATOCYTE /nee-**ma**-to-siyt/ See *cnidocyte*.

NEMATOPHORE /nee-**ma**-to-for/ A diminutive *dactylozooid* (defensive *polyp*) of *Plumularia* and related genera (CNIDARIA-**Hydrozoa**). Synonymous with "sarcostyle."

NEPHRIDIOPORE /ne-**frid**-ee-o-por/ The external opening of a *nephridium*.

NEPHRIDIUM /ne-**frid**-ee-uhm/ **pl. nephridia** /ne-**frid**-ee-uh/ An *osmoregulatory* and/or *excretory* organ in invertebrates that consists of a *ciliated* collecting area and a tube that leads to the outside. Nephridia can be fused with *coelomoducts*, but they are derived from *ectoderm*. The evolution and homology—and thus the terminology and taxonomic occurrences—of different types of nephridia and their parts are debated, which results in some variation in usage. See also *metanephridium*, *mixonephridium*, and *protonephridium*, as well as *nephridiopore* and *flame cell*.

NEPHROZOA /nef-ro-**zo**-ah/ Name for the clade that contains Chaetognatha, the *protostomes*, and the *deuterostomes* (that is, all *animals* except Porifera, Cnidaria, Ctenophora, and Xenacoelomorpha [*xenoturbellids* and *acoelomorphs*]).

NERVE NET The disorganized network of nerve cells under the *epidermis*, and sometimes under the *gastrodermis*, of cnidarians; the cells are "nonpolar" (i.e., action potentials can proceed in different directions along them) (CNIDARIA). Synonymous with "plexus."

NEUROPODIUM /nyoor-o-**po**-dee-uhm/ The ventral lobe of a *parapodium* (ANNELIDA-**Polychaeta**). See also *notopodium*.

NEUROSECRETORY /**nyoo**-ro-**see**-**kre**-to-ree/ Describing neurons or neural tissues that produce chemicals in response to excitation from other neurons.

NIDAMENTAL GLAND /ni-dah-**men**-tal …/ Generally, a *gland* that secretes the matrix and protective covering for an assemblage of fertilized eggs (i.e., an *egg* capsule), noted among invertebrates mostly in mollusks, primarily in squid (especially MOLLUSCA-**Cephalopoda**).

NITROGENOUS WASTE /niy-**trah**-jen-uhs …/ The toxic, nitrogen-containing byproducts of protein and nucleic-acid metabolism, which are removed from organisms mainly via the *excretion* of ammonia, *urea*, or *uric acid*, depending on the availability of water. See also *excretion*, *kidney*, *Malpighian tubules*, *nephridium*, and *renette cells*.

NOTOCHORD /**no**-to-kord/ In chordates, a rubbery extension of cartilage-like tissue that runs under the dorsal nerve cord; in tunicates it is present only in the *larvae* (CHORDATA).

NOTOPODIUM /no-to-**po**-dee-uhm/ The dorsal lobe of a *parapodium* (ANNELIDA-**Polychaeta**). See also *neuropodium.*

NOTUM /**no**-tuhm/ In general, the dorsal region; notably, in insects, it is the name of the dorsal *sclerite* of the *thorax* (especially ARTHROPODA-HEXAPODA-**Insecta**). See also *tergite* and *tergum.*

NYMPH /nimf/ An immature stage that, in overall morphology, is similar in appearance to the *adult*; it is used especially for young *ametabolous* or *hemimetabolous* insects (ARTHROPODA-HEXAPODA-**Insecta**), arachnids (ARTHROPODA-CHELICERATA-**Arachnida** especially -Acari), and myriapods (ARTHROPODA-MYRIAPODA).

OCELLUS /o-**sel**-uhs/ A type of *eye* that can range from a few *photoreceptors* under a field of pigments (i.e., an *eyespot*) to an aggregation of nerves and a *cuticular* lens; it may originate from *epidermal* cells with *cilia* or *microvilli.*

ODONTOPHORE /o-**don**-tuh-for/ Cartilage-like mass that underlies and supports the *radula* of gastropods (MOLLUSCA-**Gastropoda**).

OLYNTHUS /o-**lin**-thuhs/ In *sponges*, the developmental stage after the *amphiblastula* has settled, and the opening formed by the *invagination* of the *flagellated* cells closes (PORIFERA).

OMMATIDIA /o-ma-**tid**-ee-ah/ The rod-like structures that compose a *compound eye*; upon entering an ommatidium, light travels first through a "cornea" (which acts as a lens), then through a "crystalline cone" (a second lens), and finally into a ring *photoreceptive* cells connected to nerve cells (ARTHROPODA).

ONCOMIRACIDIUM /on-ko-**meer**-ah-**sid**-ee-uhm/ The *larva* of a *monogenetic fluke*; it is a free-swimming, *ciliated larva* that has adhesive *glands* used in attaching to the new host (PLATYHELMINTHES-**Monogenea**).

ONCOSPHERE /on-ko-sfeer/ In *tapeworms*, a *hexacanth larva* encased in at least one *embryonic envelope* (PLATYHELMINTHES-**Cestoda**).

OOCYST /o-o-sist/ The stage of *malaria* (*Plasmodium*) that arises after the joining of the *gamonts* and which is embedded in the *stomach* wall of the mosquito ([PROTISTA-CHROMALVEOLATA-STRAMENOPILES-APICOMPLEXA-ACONOIDASIDA-HAEMOSPORORIDA]-*Plasmodium*).

OOCYTE /o-o-siyt/ A cell that undergoes meiosis to produce an *ovum* (*egg*). The "primary oocyte" is *diploid* and undergoes meiosis I to produce the "secondary oocyte" which is thus *haploid*. The secondary oocyte undergoes meiosis II to produce the *ovum*.

OOECIUM /o-o-**ee**-si-uhm/ See *ovicell*.

OOTYPE /o-o-tiyp/ In *flukes*, the chamber in the female reproductive system where the *seminal receptacle, yolk gland*, and *ovary* connect; this is where the *egg* is assembled (PLATYHELMINTHES-**Trematoda**).

OOZOID /o-o-**zo**-id/ An individual that develops from a *zygote* but reproduces asexually, eventually *budding* off sexual individuals to complete the cycle (CHORDATA-TUNICATA-**Thaliacea**-Doliolida, -Salpida, CNIDARIA).

OPEN CIRCULATORY SYSTEM A circulatory system in which *blood* or *hemolymph* travels through vessels from the heart to *sinuses* (body cavities) and does not return to the heart via a capillary network (ARTHROPODA, CHORDATA-TUNICATA, HEMICHORDATA, MOLLUSCA-[except for **Cephalopoda**]; no circulatory system present in [ACANTHOCEPHALA], CNIDARIA, ECTOPROCTA, ENTOPROCTA [probably], NEMATODA, PLATYHELMINTHES, PORIFERA, ROTIFERA). See also *closed circulatory system*, *hemocoel*, and *ostium*.

OPERCULUM /o-**per**-kyoo-luhm/ A lid, such as that used by some *snails* to cover the opening of their *shells*, or the flap that covers the *tympanum* in some insects (cicadas).

OPHIOPLUTEUS /o-fee-o-**ploo**-tee-uhs/ The *larval* stage of ophiuroids that is after the *pluteus* stage and has long, internally-supported arms and develops without attaching to the substrate (ECHINODERMATA-**Ophiuroidea**).

OPISTHOMA or OPISTHOSOMA /o-**pis**-tho-mah or o-**pis**-tho-**so**-mah/ A organism's posterior section, which usually contains the digestive, reproductive, and respiratory organs; used almost exclusively for chelicertates (ARTHROPODA-CHELICERATA) but also for pogonophorans (ANNELIDA-**Polychaeta**-Canalipalpata-Siboglinidae). Texts exist where both versions of this term are used interchangeably, or one version or the other is used alongside "*abdomen*;" among arachnologists, *opisthoma* appears to be more commonly used in studies of spiders (-**Arachnida**-Araneae) and ticks and mites (-Acari).

ORAL 1. Pertaining to the *mouth*. Synonymous with "buccal." 2. The side of an echinoderm that has the *mouth* (or the *mouth* and *anus* in *irregular echinoids*) (ECHINODERMATA).

ORAL ARMS Extensions of tissue around the *mouths* of scyphozoan *medusae*, *homologous* to the *manubrium* in other *medusae*; they have *cnidocytes* and can capture prey, and they collect food from the *food pouches* and *tentacles* around the margin of the *bell* (CNIDARIA-**Scyphozoa**).

ORAL CAVITY See *buccal cavity*.

ORAL SIPHON or **ORAL CANAL** See *buccal siphon/canal*.

ORGAN OF VERRILL, ORGANS OF VERRILL, or **VERRILL'S ORGAN** /… ver-ril/ See *funnel organ*.

ORGANELLE /or-gan-**el**/ A specialized, segregated structure within a single cell; if referring to an internal body in *eukaryotic* cells, the organelle usually has a double membrane covering.

ORGAN-PIPE CORAL Common name for *Tubipora*, a "soft *coral*" that, oddly, has a skeleton made of calcium carbonate (CNIDARIA-**Anthozoa-Octocorallia**-Alcyonacea).

OSCULUM /**ahs**-kyoo-luhm/ In *asconoid* and *syconoid sponges*, the opening through which water leaves the *spongocoel*; in *leuconoid sponges*, an opening through which water leaves interior *flagellated chambers* of the body via an *excurrent canal* (PORIFERA).

OSMOREGULATION /**ahs**-mo-reg-yoo-**lay**-shuhn/ The active control by an organism of its water content.

OSPHRADIUM /ahs-**fray**-dee-uhm/ A sensory structure near the *gills* in the *mantle cavity* of many gastropods; it is mainly a *chemoreceptor* but can also detect sediment concentrations (MOLLUSCA-**Gastropoda**).

OSSICLES /**ahs**-si-kuhlz/ Internal *calcareous* deposits, usually derived from *mesoderm*; in echinoderms (ECHINODERMATA) they can fit together to make an internal skeleton, be highly reduced, or modified into spines; in crustaceans (ARTHROPODA-CRUSTACEA), they can act as attachment sites for muscles associated with the *alimentary canal*.

OSTIUM /**ahs**-tee-uhm/ 1. Opening through which *blood* returns to the *heart* from the *hemocoel* (ARTHROPODA-HEXAPODA-**Insecta**). 2. A pore through which water enters a *sponge* (PORIFERA).

OVARY /**o**-vuh-ree/ An organ that produces *ova* (*eggs*) and often certain sex hormones. See also *gamete* and *gonad*.

OVICELL /**o**-vi-sel/ *Zooid* in ectoproct colonies that is specialized for brooding *eggs* (ECTOPROCTA-**Gymnolaemata**-Cheilostomata-*Bugula*). Synonymous with "ooecium."

OVIDUCT /**o**-vee-duhkt/ The duct that carries *ova* from the *ovary*.

OVIGEROUS LEGS /o-**vi**-jer-uhs …/ In male *sea spiders*, the first pair of *legs*, which are modified to carry *eggs*; they are smaller than the other *legs* (ARTHROPODA-CHELICERATA-**Pycnogonida**).

OVIPARY /o-**vip**-uh-ree/ Mode of reproduction in which the *embryo* develops inside an *egg* that is released by the mother before the *embryo* completes development. See also *ovovivipary* and *vivipary*.

OVIPOSITOR /o-vi-**pah**-zi-tor/ A distinct, medial organ used by females to place *eggs* in their optimal setting for survival and development, commonly found in terrestrial arthropods that require *eggs* to be laid inside host plants or *animals*, the soil, or dead wood.

OVOTESTES /o-vo-**tes**-tees/ The *gonad* of certain *snails*; it can produce both *eggs* and *sperm* at different times during the *animal's* lifetime (MOLLUSCA-**Gastropoda**- [OPISTHOBRANCHIA], -[PULMONATA]).

OVOVIVIPARY /o-vo-viy-**vip**-uh-ree/ Mode of reproduction in which the *embryo* develops within an *egg* membrane, but this is retained within the mother, and the offspring leaves her as a *juvenile*. Synonymous with "ovipary" and "ovoviviparity." See also *ovipary* and *vivipary*.

OVUM /o-vuhm/ **pl. ova** /o-vah/ The product of division of the secondary *oocyte*. Synonymous with *egg*.

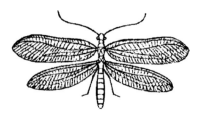

P

PALLIAL LINE /**pal**-li-ahl …/ The mark on the ventral edge (i.e., around the opening, opposite the *umbo*) of a bivalve *shell* made by the *pallial muscle* and indicating the extent of the *nacre* (MOLLUSCA-**Bivalvia**). Synonymous with "pallial groove."

PALLIAL MUSCLE /**pal**-li-ahl …/ One of the muscles that attaches the *mantle* of a bivalve to its *shell* (MOLLUSCA-**Bivalvia**).

PALP /palp/ 1. Any *appendage* near the *mouth* used as a sensory organ, especially the *maxillary palps* and *labial palps* of crustaceans, insects, and myriapods (ARTHROPODA-CRUSTACEA, -HEXAPODA, -MYRIAPODA), as well as the *labial palps* of certain *clams* and *snails* (MOLLUSCA-**Bivalvia**, -**Gastropoda**). 2. Short for *pedipalps*, the second pair of *appendages* in chelicerates (ARTHROPODA-CHELICERATA).

PANCREAS Although it has a specific structure in vertebrates, this term has sometimes been used to refer to any *digestive gland* in invertebrates.

PAPILLA /pah-**pil**-luh/ **pl. papillae** /pah-**pil**-lee/ Any small, fleshy projection usually used as a sensory structure; diminutive of *papula*.

PAPULA /**pa**-pyoo-luh/ **pl. papulae** /**pa**-pyoo-lee/ In asteroids, a tiny extension of the *coelom* through the *test* on the *aboral* surface, used in respiration; Latin for "swelling" (ECHINODERMATA-**Asteroidea**). See also *papilla* and *paxillae*.

PARAMYLON /peyr-ah-**miy**-lahn/ Type of starch that is created in the *pyrenoids* of *Euglena* and related *protists*, and which is stored inside their cells as large, capsule-shaped granules called "paramylon bodies" ([PROTISTA-EXCAVATA-EUGLENOZOA-EUGLENIDA]).

PARAPHYLETIC /**peyr**-uh-fiy-**le**-tik/ Describing a group of taxa whose members all descend from a common ancestor but is missing the most recently evolved descendants of that ancestor.

PARAPODIA /peyr-ah-**po**-dee-ah/ **sing. parapodium** /peyr-ah-**po**-dee-uhm/ The paired *appendages* of polychaetes; they consist of two lobes (the *neuropodium* and *notopodium*), are supported by *acicula*, bear *setae*, and are used in respiration and locomotion; there are two for every *segment* (ANNELIDA-**Polychaeta**).

PARASITISM Relationship between two species in which one benefits while the other is harmed. See also *symbiosis*.

PARENCHYMA /peyr-**ren**-kah-mah/ 1. The tissue in *acoelomates* that fills the space between the *epidermis* and the *alimentary canal* (for example PLATYHELMINTHES). 2. The cells of an organ that define its function.

PARENCHYMULA /peyr-ren-**kiy**-myoo-lah/ One of two main *larval* types in *sponges* after the *stomoblastula* turns inside out (the other being the *amphiblastula*); after this change, the *flagella* point outward, and the ball fills up with undifferentiated cells which arise, at least in part, from *flagellated* cells that migrate to the inside (PORIFERA).

PARIETAL MUSCLES /puh-**riy**-e-tuhl …/ Muscles that connect the lateral and frontal walls of ectoproct *zooids*. When they contract, the *lophophore* is pushed out (ECTOPROCTA).

PARTHENOGENESIS /**par**-then-o-**je**-ne-sis/ Mode of asexual reproduction whereby development begins without the *egg* being fertilized by a *sperm*.

PAXILLAE /pak-**sil**-lee/ **sing. paxilla** /pak-**sil**-lah/ The umbrella-like *ossicles* of burrowing asteroids that keep sand and other debris away from the skin while allowing water to pass over the *papulae* (ECHINODERMATA-**Asteroidea**).

PEDAL DISC /**pee**-dahl …/ In *sea anemones*, the base of the body column that attaches the *animal* to the substrate and can be used for locomotion (CNIDARIA-**Anthozoa**).

PEDICEL /**ped**-i-sel/ Any constriction that connects an organ, *appendage*, body section, or nest. See also *peduncle*, *petiole*, *stalk*, and *stolon*.

PEDICELLARIA /ped-i-sel-**lar**-ee-ah/ In some echinoderms, the tiny *appendages* on the body that clean and protect the outer covering of the *animal*; they terminate in *jaw*-like, scissor-like, or pincer-like structures that constantly remove *larvae* and debris (ECHINODERMATA-**Asteroidea**, -**Echinoidea**).

PEDIPALPS /**pe**-dee-palps/ In chelicerates, the second pair of *appendages*; especially referred to in arachnids, where they have evolved morphologies for prey capture and manipulation, as well as reproduction (ARTHROPODA-CHELICERATA especially -**Arachnida**).

PEDUNCLE /pe-**duhn**-kuhl/ 1. Any constriction that connects an organ, *appendage*, body section, or nest. 2. The preferred term for the elongate attaching structure of a *barnacle* (ARTHROPODA-CRUSTACEA-**Maxillopoda-Cirripedia**). See also *pedicel, petiole, stalk*, and *stolon*.

PELAGIC /pah-**la**-jik/ Describing ocean or lake surface water far from shore, as well as the organisms that live there.

PELLICLE /**pel**-li-kuhl/ The tough but flexible proteinaceous layer below the cell membrane in many *protists*, often arranged in a spiral pattern ([PROTISTA]).

PELTA /**pel**-tah/ Crescent-shaped bundle of *microtubules* around the *basal body* in some *protists* ([PROTISTA-EXCAVATA, especially -FORNICATA-EOPHARYNGIA-DIPLOMONADIDA, -FORNICATA-EOPHARYNGIA-RETORTAMONADIDA, -PREAXOSTYLA-OXYMONADIDA, -PARABASALIA]). See also *pelta-axostyle complex*.

PELTA-AXOSTYLE COMPLEX /**pel**-tah **ak**-so-stiyl …/ In some *protists*, the combination of a *pelta* and *axostyle* (two *microtubule* structures) ([PROTISTA-EXCAVATA, especially -FORNICATA-EOPHARYNGIA-DIPLOMONADIDA, -FORNICATA-EOPHARYNGIA-RETORTAMONADIDA, -PREAXOSTYLA-OXYMONADIDA, -PARABASALIA]).

PEN See *gladius*.

PENIS An intromittent organ for transferring *sperm* that, unlike a *cirrus*, is not eversible.

PENTACRINOID LARVA /pen-tah-**kriy**-noyd …/ In crinoids, the *larval* stage that follows settlement of the *vitellaria* and resembles a miniature *stalked* crinoid; the

crown may break free to settle elsewhere
(ECHINODERMATA-**Crinoidea**).

PENTACTULA /pen-**tak**-chyoo-lah/ In some *sea cucumbers*,
the final *larval* stage after the *vitellaria* or *doliolaria* has
developed *buccal podia* (ECHINODERMATA-
Holothuroidea).

PEREIOPOD /puh-**ray**-uh-pahd, puh-**ree**-uh-pahd, or puh-
riy-uh-pahd/ In crustaceans, a *thoracopod* used for
grasping the substrate, walking, or swimming (as opposed
to the food-handling *maxillipeds*) (ARTHROPODA-
CRUSTACEA). Sometimes spelled "pereopods" or
"peraeopods;" from "pereion," the term used for
crustacean *thoracic segments* that are not fused with the head
and often bear *legs*.

PERICARDIUM /peyr-ah-**kar**-dee-uhm/ The fluid-filled
cavity of *coelomic* origin that surrounds the *heart*.

PERIOSTRACUM /peyr-ee-**ahs**-trah-kuhm/ The
outermost layer of a molluscan *shell*; it is proteinaceous
and usually thin or absent (MOLLUSCA).

PERISARC /**peyr**-ee-sark/ The proteinaceous covering
secreted by the *epidermis* of the colonial hydrozoan
coenosarc (CNIDARIA-**Hydrozoa**).

PERITONEUM /**peyr**-i-to-**nee**-uhm/ The *mesodermally*
derived tissue lining the body cavity and organs in
coelomate animals.

PERITROPHIC MEMBRANE /peyr-ee-**tro**-fik …/ In
insects, the thin layer of *cuticle* that surrounds the food as it
passes through the *midgut*; it is permeable to enzymes and
nutrients (ARTHROPODA-HEXAPODA-**Insecta**).

PERIVISCERAL COELOM /peyr-ee-**vis**-ser-ahl .../ A true *coelom*, or parts of one, that surrounds the *alimentary canal*.

PERRADIAL CANALS /pur-**ray**-dee-ahl .../ In scyphozoan *medusae*, those *radial canals* that form a branching network connecting the *ring canal* to the *stomach* (CNIDARIA-**Scyphozoa**). See also *adradial canals* and *interradial canals*.

PETIOLE /**pet**-ee-ol/ Any constriction that connects an organ, *appendage*, body section, or nest. See also *pedicel*, *peduncle*, *stalk*, and *stolon*.

PHAGOCYTOSIS /**fa**-go-si-**to**-sis/ Type of ingestion by a single cell in which a piece of food is surrounded by plasma membrane, engulfed, and pinched off to make a food vacuole; the vacuole will join with a "lysosome" (an *organelle* that carries enzymes) for the food to be digested. See *pinocytosis*.

PHARYNGEAL BASKET /fah-**rin**-jee-ahl .../ The enlarged, sieve-like *pharynx* of tunicates, used in filtering food (CHORDATA-TUNICATA).

PHARYNGEAL SLITS /fah-**rin**-jee-ahl .../ Elongate holes in the *pharynges* of chordates and hemichordates; in the invertebrate groups water passes through these holes and returns to the environment, leaving behind food, which is swallowed (CHORDATA-CEPHALOCHORDATA, -TUNICATA, HEMICHORDATA). "Gill slits" is often used interchangeably with "pharyngeal slits" among the invertebrate groups, but only among the hemichordates is the passage of water through the *pharynx* the primary mode of gas exchange; cephalochordates and tunicates perform gas exchange across various tissues in contact with the environment. It is most notably among the

vertebrates where pharyngeal slits have been highly
modified into such structures as *gill* supports in fish.

PHARYNX /**feyr**-inks/ **pl. pharynges** /fuh-**rin**-jeez/ A
muscular region of the *alimentary canal* directly after the
mouth; it is often modified as a food-processing device,
such as the *mastax* of rotifers (ROTIFERA) or the
pharyngeal basket of tunicates (CHORDATA-TUNICATA).

PHASMID /**faz**-mid/ 1. A posterior structure in nematodes
that may function as a *chemoreceptor* (NEMATODA). See
also *amphid*. 2. Alternative common name for a "stick
insect" (ARTHROPODA-HEXAPODA-**Insecta**-
Phasmatodea).

PHOTORECEPTOR /**fo**-to-ree-**sep**-tuhr/ Any organ, cell,
or subcellular structure used to sense light.

PHYLLOPODIUM /**fi**-lo-**po**-dee-uhm/ A flat crustacean
appendage that is used to move water during swimming
and respiration, or for moving food; not necessarily
attached to the *thorax* (that is, not necessarily a *thoracopod*)
(ARTHROPODA-CRUSTACEA). See also *stenopodium*.

PHYLOGENETICS /**fiy**-lo-je-**ne**-tiks/ The study of
historical relationships among organisms, resulting in
hypothetical reconstructions of their evolution. See also
systematics.

PHYLOGENY /fiy-**lah**-juh-nee/ A branching diagram
illustrating the historical relationships among groups of
organisms.

PILIDIUM LARVA /pi-**li**-dee-uhm .../ The cap-like *larva*
of nemerteans (NEMERTEA).

PINACOCYTE /pi-**na**-ko-siyt/ Type of *sponge* cell that covers the outside of the *animal* to make the *pinacoderm* and provides a variety of functions (PORIFERA).

PINACODERM /pi-**na**-ko-duhrm/ The outer layer of *sponges*, which is composed of *pinacocytes* and has functions similar to the *epidermis* in other phyla; it adheres the *animal* to the substrate, is slightly contractile, and can to some degree line internal passageways (before being met by the *choanoderm*) (PORIFERA).

PINOCYTOSIS /**pi**-no-siy-**to**-sis/ Type of cellular digestion like *phagocytosis*, but in which the nutrients are in liquid form, and the vacuole does not join with a lysosome (an *organelle* that carries enzymes).

PINWORMS Common name for a family of tiny, *parasitic* nematodes; *Enterobius vermicularius* is the species that infects humans (NEMATODA-Oxyuridae).

PLANKTON /**plank**-tuhn/ Aquatic organisms, usually microscopic and *pelagic*, that move with the ocean currents.

PLANULA /**plan**-yoo-lah/ The cnidarian *larva* that follows a *stereogastrula* and becomes either a *polyp* or an *actinula*; it is *ciliated* and has sensory cells and *cnidocytes* (CNIDARIA).

PLASMALEMMA /**plaz**-mah-**lem**-mah/ Another term for the cell membrane (the flexible, semi-fluid, lipid layer that encloses an individual cell).

PLEOPOD /**plee**-o-pahd/ In crustaceans, an *abdominal appendage* (ARTHROPODA-CRUSTACEA). From "pleon," an alternative term for the *abdomen* of crustaceans; see also *thoracopod* and *uropod*.

PLEROCERCOID /pleyr-ro-**ser**-koyd/ *Larval* form of *tapeworms* that develops from the *procercoid larva*; it is the stage that becomes the *adult* in the *definitive host* (PLATYHELMINTHES-**Cestoda**). See also *hexacanth*.

PLEURON /**plur**-ahn/ In general, a lateral region of a body, or in arthropods, a *sclerite* covering this region, especially on the *thorax* of insects (ARTHROPODA).

PLEXUS /**plek**-suhs/ See *nerve net.*

PLUTEUS /**ploo**-tee-uhs/ *Bilaterally symmetrical* echinoderm *larva* after the *gastrula* that gives rise to the *echinopluteus* or *ophiopluteus* stage (ECHINODERMATA-**Echinoidea**, -**Ophiuroidea**).

PNEUMATOPHORE /noo-**mat**-to-for/ In some free-living hydrozoan colonies, a specialized structure that contains gas. It develops from the *planula*, and keeps the colony of *polyps* afloat; it is usually filled with nitrogen, although it may contain high quantities of inert gases (CNIDARIA-**Hydrozoa**-Siphonophorae). See also *Portuguese man-of-war.*

PNEUMATOSTOME /noo-**mat**-to-stom/ In pulmonate gastropods, the opening to the highly modified, lung-like *mantle cavity* (MOLLUSCA-**Gastropoda**-[PULMONATA]).

PODIUM /**po**-dee-uhm/ See *tube foot.*

POISON CLAWS See *fangs* (2).

POLAR FIELD One of two patches of *cilia* extending out on either side of the *aboral* sense organ of ctenophores (CTENOPHORA).

POLIAN VESICLE /**po**-lee-ahn **ve**-si-kahl/ A type of internal outpocketing of the *ring canal* in most echinoderms; it is used in regulating the fluid pressure of the *water vascular system* (ECHINODERMATA except **Crinoidea**).

POLYP /**pah**-lip/ The life cycle stage in cnidarians that is usually non-reproductive and *sessile*, and often colonial (CNIDARIA).

POLYPHYLETIC /**pah**-lee-fiy-**le**-tik/ Describing a group of taxa whose members descend from different ancestors and are not as closely related as their taxonomic grouping implies.

POLYPIDE /**pah**-lee-piyd/ The digestive and food-gathering tissues, as well as supporting muscles and nerves, of an ectoproct *zooid* (ECTOPROCTA). See also *brown body.*

POLYPLOID /**pah**-lee-ployd/ n. **polyploidy** /**pah**-lee-ploy-dee/ Describing cells or organisms that have more than two copies of each chromosome, some usually being exact copies (especially [PROTISTA-CHROMALVEOLATA-STRAMENOPILES-CILIOPHORA]). See also *diploid* and *haploid.*

PORE PLATE Specialized area of the wall between neighboring *zooids* of a colonial ectoproct; it bears several openings and allows materials to pass between the *zooids* (ECTOPROCTA).

POROCYTE /**por**-o-siyt/ Type of *sponge* cell embedded in the *pinacoderm* that surrounds and controls an *ostium* (PORIFERA).

PORTUGUESE MAN-OF-WAR Common name for the
dangerous, floating, colonial hydrozoan species in the
genus *Physalia* (CNIDARIA-**Hydrozoa**-Siphonophorae-
Physaliidae-*Physalia*).

POSTABDOMEN In scorpions, the elongate posterior
segments that terminate in a stinger (ARTHROPODA-
CHELICERATA-**Arachnida**-Scorpiones). (Written as
"post-abdomen," this term is also used for certain
sections of the *test* following the *abdomen* in some
radiolarian *protists* [PROTISTA-RHIZARIA-
RADIOLARIA-POLYCYSTINA-NASSELLARIA].)
Synonymous with "metasoma" in scorpions.

POST-ANAL TAIL A posterior extension of the body,
past the *anus*, which was one of the defining features of
chordates. It is clearly seen in vertebrates, cephalochordates
and the *larvae* of tunicates. It seems to appear also in one
family of hemichordates, and recent molecular phylogenies
place this phyulum as sister to the echinoderms
(CHORDATA-CEPHALOCHORDATA, -TUNICATA,
HEMICHORDATA-Harrimaniidae).

POSTLARVA See *megalops*.

PRAYING MANTID or PRAYING MANTIS Common
name for a member of the insect order Mantodea, often
misspelled as "preying mantid/mantis;" although they do
hunt and capture prey, they do so with *subchelate* front
legs that resemble praying hands; the difference between
"mantid" and "mantis" is that the former is derived from
the family name Mantidae and the latter from the genus
name *Mantis*, although there are species outside both of
these groups in Mantodea that take the general form of a
praying mantid (ARTHROPODA-HEXAPODA-
Insecta-Mantodea).

PRISMATIC LAYER /priz-**ma**-tik …/ The *calcareous* layer of a molluscan *shell* beneath the *periostracum* in which the material is arranged in vertical crystals; it is the layer responsible for the colors and patterns on most *shells* (MOLLUSCA).

PROBOSCIS /pro-**bahs**-sis/ Any protruding, extensible elongation of the *mouth* or *pharynx*, or elongation of the head, usually used to assist in feeding.

PROCERCOID /pro-**ser**-koyd/ *Larval* form of *tapeworms* that develops from the *oncosphere* (the enveloped *hexacanth*); it enters the *intestine* of the *intermediate host* and then enters the *definitive host* to become the *plerocercoid* (PLATYHELMINTHES-**Cestoda**).

PROCUTICLE /**pro**-**kyoo**-ti-kuhl/ The inner layer of arthropod *exoskeletons* that lies just under the *epicuticle* (ARTHROPODA).

PROECDYSIS /**pro**-ek-**diy**-sis/ Stage of arthropod *molting* during which the *animal* prepares to shed its old *exoskeleton*; the *exoskeleton* separates from the new *epidermis* underneath, and *ecdysone* increases in concentration; in crustaceans, the *blood* absorbs calcium from the *exoskeleton* and makes *gastroliths* (ARTHROPODA). Also called "pre-ecdysis" or "premolt." See also *anecdysis*, *ecdysis*, and *metecdysis*.

PROGLOTTID /pro-**glah**-tid/ One of the reproductive sections of an *adult tapeworm*. Proglottids contain the sex organs, and as they fill with mature *eggs*, they break off and pass out with the host's *feces* (PLATYHELMINTHES-**Cestoda**).

PROLEGS Legs on the *abdominal segments* of insect *larvae*, especially *caterpillars*; in the latter they have internal muscles and are tipped with structures for grasping the substrate (*crochets*) (ARTHROPODA-HEXAPODA-**Insecta** especially -Lepidoptera).

PROSOMA /pro-**so**-mah/ In *chelicerates*, the anterior section of the organism, which usually has the sense organs, *mouth*, and six pairs of *appendages* (ARTHROPODA-CHELICERATA).

PROSOPYLE /**pro**-so-piyl/ In *sponges*, the opening through which water passes from an *incurrent canal* to a *flagellated chamber* (PORIFERA).

PROSTOMIUM /pro-**sto**-mee-uhm/ In polychaetes, the fleshy flap that is anterior to the *mouth* and bears the *eyes*, *antennae*, and *palps* (ANNELIDA-**Polychaeta**).

PROTANDRIC /pro-**tan**-drik/ Type of *hermaphroditism* in which individuals change their sex over time, starting as male and later becoming female. See also *protogynous*.

PROTISTS /**pro**-tists/ Informal term for single-celled *eukaryotes* in which the unicellular condition is not secondarily derived (thus excluding the various organisms called "yeast," which are unicellular fungi); these were previously grouped into the kingdom Protista, which is now known to be *polyphyletic*; it includes colonial organisms, some of which form large bodies with specialized tissues and structures, although in some previous classification schemes the largest forms (such as kelp and slime molds) were excluded.

PROTOCEREBRUM /pro-to-ser-**ree**-bruhm/ Section of the arthropod brain that receives information from the *eyes* and integrates movement (ARTHROPODA). See also *deuterocerebrum* and *tritocerebrum*.

PROTOGYNOUS /pro-to-**jiy**-nuhs or pro-to-**giy**-nuhs/ Type of *hermaphroditism* in which individuals change their sex over time, starting as female and later becoming male. See also *protandric*.

PROTOMERITE /pro-to-**mer**-iyt/ In gregarines that *parasitize* insects and crustaceans, the anterior part of the cell that bears the *epimerite* ([PROTISTA-CHROMALVEOLATA-STRAMENOPILES-APICOMPLEXA-CONOIDASIDA-GREGARINASINA]). See also *deutomerite* and *epimerite*.

PROTONEPHRIDIUM /pro-to-ne-**fri**-dee-uhm/ A *nephridium* that does not use a funnel-shaped collecting structure inside the coelom but rather a closed sac that ends in one or more *flame cells*. The sac has perforations, and the beating of the *flame cells(s)* brings unwanted fluid into the nephridium and moves it to the outside. See also *metanephridium* and *mixonephridium*.

PROTOPOD /**pro**-to-pahd/ See *protopodite*.

PROTOPODITE /pro-to-**po**-diyt/ The proximal, basal part of a *biramous* arthropod *appendage* that gives rise to the two main *rami* (ARTHROPODA-CHELICERATA-**Merostomata**-Xiphosura, -CRUSTACEA, -TRILOBITA). Also written as "protopod." See also *biramous*.

PROTOSTOME /**pro**-to-stom/ **adj. protostomatous** /pro-to-**sto**-mah-tuhs/ A *triploblastic animal* that has a type of *embryological* development in which the *blastopore* becomes the *mouth* ([ACANTHOCEPHALA],

ANNELIDA, ARTHROPODA, BRACHIOPODA, CHAETOGNATHA, CYCLIOPHORA, ECTOPROCTA, ENTOPROCTA, GASTROTRICHA, GNATHOSTOMULIDA, LORICIFERA, KINORHYNCHA, MICROGNATHOZOA, MOLLUSCA, NEMATODA, NEMATOMORPHA, NEMERTEA, ONYCHOPHORA, PHORONIDA, PRIAPULIDA, PLATYHELMINTHES, ROTIFERA, TARDIGRADA). The fate of the *blastopore* in *lophophorates*, and thus whether they are truly protostomes, has been debated. However, they place firmly among known protostomes in molecular *phylogenies*, and the term (as well as *"deuterostome"*) is applied to all descendants of an ancestor so described, even if the feature has been secondarily modified. Protostomes appear to be monophyletic and divided in three clades: *Ecdysozoa*, *Spiralia*, and Chaetognatha. See also *deuterostome*.

PROTOSTYLE /**pro-to**-stiyl/ In bivalves and gastropods, the mucous rod secreted by a groove in the anterior part of the *intestine* and used in digestion; it is rotated and contains enzymes like a *crystalline style* but is composed mostly of mucous (MOLLUSCA-**Bivalvia**, -**Gastropoda**).

PROTOTROCII /**pro-to-trahk**/ One of two *ciliated* bands around the middle of a *trochophore larva*, this one located away from the *anus*. See also *metatroch*.

PSEUDOCHITIN /**soo-do-kiy**-tin/ See *tectin*.

PSEUDOCOELOMATE /**soo-do-see**-lo-mayt/ A type of body plan in which the body cavity is not derived from *mesoderm*; thus the cavity and its organs are not lined completely with muscle (it is missing from around the organs and the *alimentary canal*), and there is no *peritoneum*

([ACANTHOCEPHALA], ENTOPROCTA, GASTROTRICHA, KINORHYNCHA, LORICIFERA, MICROGNATHOZOA, NEMATODA, NEMATOMORPHA, PRIAPULIDA, ROTIFERA). Having a pseudocoelom was once believed to be informative of evolutionary relationships, and the pseudocoelomate phyla were previously referred to collectively as "Aschelminthes" or "Pseudocoelomata." However, it is now clear from molecular phylogenies that the pseudocoelomate condition has evolved independently several times, and that phyla do not group by *coelom* development. See also *acoelomate* and *coelom*.

PSEUDOPODIUM or PSEUDOPOD /soo-do-**po**-dee-uhm or **soo**-do-pahd/ **pl. pseudopodia or pseudopods** /soo-do-**po**-dee-ah or **soo**-do-pahdz/ A temporary protrusion of a single cell used for movement and ingesting food (especially [PROTISTA-AMOEBOZOA-TUBULINEA-TUBULINIDA] for example -*Amoeba*). See also *axopodium*, *filopodium*, *lobopodium*, and *reticulopodium*.

PTYCHOCYST /**tik**-o-sist/ Type of *cnidocyst* characterized by having a thread that, in the undischarged state, has pleats around its circumference but no helical or lengthwise folds; this creates a thread which, at rest, is flattened but not shortened (CNIDARIA). See also *nematocyst* and *spirocyst*.

PUPA /**pyoo**-pah/ **pl. pupae** /**pyoo**-pee/ The inactive stage in *holometabolous* insects between *larva* and *adult* during which the internal tissues are broken down and reorganized to make new mouthparts, reproductive structures, and wings (ARTHROPODA-HEXAPODA-**Insecta**). See also *metamorphosis*.

PYGIDIUM /pi-**ji**-dee-uhm/ A distinct, posterior end part in many invertebrates that is not a *metamere* but which bears the *anus*; the term is commonly used with annelids and arthropods (especially ANNELIDA, ARTHROPODA). See also *telson*.

PYLORIC CECUM /piy-**lor**-ik **see**-kuhm/ Any one of the outpocketings of the *pyloric stomach* of *sea stars* in which most nutrient absorption takes place (ECHINODERMATA-**Asteroidea**). Also called "digestive cecum," "hepatic cecum," or "digestive gland" (although the latter has a more general definition, see *digestive gland*).

PYLORIC STOMACH /piy-**lor**-ik .../ 1. In asteroids and ophiuroids, the more *aboral* of two main cavities in the *alimentary canal*; this *stomach* cannot be everted out of the *mouth* (ECHINODERMATA-**Asteroidea**, -Ophiuroidea). See also *cardiac stomach*. 2. Likewise, in crustaceans, the *stomach* that is further from the *mouth*, after the *cardiac stomach* (ARTHROPODA-CRUSTACEA).

PYRENOID /**piy**-re-noyd/ Subcellular structure (called such to distinguish it from a typical *organelle*, as it is not surrounded by a membrane) found in several *protists* and some primitive land plants, that concentrates carbon dioxide for use in photosynthesis. See also *paramylon*.

R

RADIAL CANAL 1. In cnidarian *medusae* (*jellyfish*), any one of the various *ciliated* channels through the *mesoglea* that connect the *ring canal* around the outer margin of the *bell* to the *gastrovascular cavities* and the *stomach* (CNIDARIA especially -**Hydrozoa**, -**Scyphozoa**). See also *adradial canals*, *interradial canals*, and *perradial canals*. 2. In echinoderms, a branch off of the *ring canal* that leads to an *arm* and gives rise to *tube feet* (ECHINODERMATA). 3. One of the elongate, *flagellated chambers* of a *syconoid sponge*.

RADIAL CLEAVAGE Type of *cleavage* in which the *blastomeres* on each level of the early *embryo* lie directly above the *blastomeres* on the lower level; usually found in *deuterostomes*, and usually associated with *indeterminate development*. See also *spiral cleavage*.

RADIAL SYMMETRY Body plan in which an organism can theoretically be divided into identical halves by cutting it along any one of an infinite number of planes through its central axis; it is common in many *sessile, filter-feeding* organisms.

RADULA /**rad**-jyoo-lah/ The basic feeding structure in mollusks, which conists of a strip of tissue covered with *chitinous* teeth (MOLLUSCA).

RAMUS /**ray**-muhs/ **pl. rami** /**ray**-mee/ Generally referring to a branch, but among invertebrates used mostly for a main branch of an arthropod *appendage*. See *biramous*, *uniramous* (ARTHROPODA).

RECTUM /**rek**-tuhm/ The section of the *alimentary canal* directly before the *anus*. See also *cloaca*.

REDIA /**re**-dee-ah/ In *digenetic flukes* the *larva* following the *sporocyst*; it has a short *alimentary canal* and *germinal cells* that give rise to the *cercariae* (PLATYHELMINTHES-**Trematoda**).

REEF Any mineralized accumulation of marine organisms so large it provides habitat for other organisms and alters the local geology. Today reefs are predominantly created by *corals* that make calcium carbonate skeletons (CNIDARIA-**Anthozoa-Hexacorallia**, especially -Scleractinia), and contributions to their structure are made by algae, mollusks, echinoderms and other *animals* with hard parts, especially those also made from calcium carbonate. Before the rise of *corals*, reefs were commonly created by cyanobacteria, glass sponges (PORIFERA-**Hexactinellida**), and other organisms with *shells*, *tests*, *spicules*, or *ossicles*, and some of these reefs continue today in particular habitats where reef-building *corals* cannot live or do not thrive (like the deep sea).

REGENERATION The ability to reproduce a severed body part; this is especially noteworthy in the turbellarians (PLATYHELMINTHES-**Turbellaria**) and the echinoderms (ECHINODERMATA). See also *autotomy*.

REGULAR ECHINOIDS /... **e**-ki-noydz/ Echinoids that are *radially symmetrical* and have their *anus* on the *aboral* surface (ECHINODERMATA-**Echinoidea** except **Irregularia**). See also *irregular echinoids*.

RENAL SAC /**ree**-nahl .../ A *bladder* at the end of the bivalve *metanephridium* that stores wastes before they leave the body (MOLLUSCA-**Bivalvia**).

RENETTE CELL /**re**-net …/ In nematodes, a type of cell used mostly in *osmoregulation* and also the *excretion* of wastes other than ammonia (NH₃); also called a "renette gland," although occurring singly or with only one other renette cell in individuals (NEMATODA). See also *flame cell.*

RENO-PERICARDIAL CANAL /**ree**-no **peyr**-ree-**kahr**-dee-uhl …/ Part of the *metanephridium* that leads from the *pericardial cavity* to the *renal sac* and which is modified for the reabsorption of useful materials.

RESPIRATORY TREE In *sea cucumbers* the highly branched *invagination* of the *cloaca* (sometimes called the *rectum* in these *animals*) that allows gas exchange between the *coelomic* fluids and sea water (ECHINODERMATA-**Holothuroidea**).

RETICULOPODIUM /re-**tik**-yoo-lo-**po**-dee-uhm/ Type of *pseudopodium* that forms a fine branching network ([PROTISTA especially -RHIZARIA-FORAMINIFERA]). Synonymous with "rhizopodium."

RHABDITES /**rab**-diyts/ The most common type of special *epidermal* secretions called *rhabdoids*; sometimes used to refer to all such secretions (PLATYHELMINTHES-**Turbellaria**).

RHABDITIFORM LARVA /rab-**dit**-uh-form …/ A *larva* of nematodes that hatches from the *egg* and is feeding and free-living; it can grow into an *adult* or give rise to a *filariform larva* (NEMATODA).

RHABDOIDS /**rab**-doydz/ Used to refer to membrane-bound *epidermal* secretions in certain phyla, and/or referring to the *glands* that make these secretions (also then written sometimes as "rhabdoid glands"), which are in the *epidermis* or underlying cells; the secretions have diverse morphologies and chemistries; they are deposited on the substrate where they likely assist in a variety of activities, such as locomotion, defense, and mating (ANNELIDA, GASTROTRICHA, NEMERTEA, especially PLATYHELMINTHES-**Turbellaria**). See also *rhabdite*, as well as *duo-gland system*.

RHIZOPODIUM /**riy**-zo-**po**-dee-uhm / See *reticulopodium*.

RHOPALIAL LAPPETS /ro-**pa**-lee-ahl lap-**pets**/ Two flaps of tissue that surround a *rhopalium* (CNIDARIA-**Cubozoa**, -**Scyphozoa**).

RHOPALIUM /ro-**pa**-lee-uhm/ In cnidarian *medusae*, one of the four or more little lobes around the margin of the *bell*. These contain clusters of neurons and control the pulsing action of the *medusa* (CNIDARIA-**Cubozoa**, -**Scyphozoa**).

RHYNCHOCOEL /**rin**-ko-seel/ The extensive *invagination* of the body wall of nemerteans in which lies the *proboscis*; it is fluid filled, and the cavity appears to be a remnant of a true *coelom* (NEMERTEA).

RIBBON WORMS The common name for nemerteans (NEMERTEA). Older names include "Rhynchocoela." See also *rhynchocoel*.

RING CANAL 1. In a cnidarian *medusa* (*jellyfish*), the extension of the *gastrovascular cavity* around the outer margin of the *bell* (CNIDARIA). Occasionally referred to as the "circumferential canal." See also *radial canal*. 2. The circumoral part of the *water vascular system* of echinoderms, off of which branch the *stone canal*, the *radial canals*, the *Polian vesicles*, and the *Tiedemann's bodies* (ECHINODERMATA).

ROSTRUM /**raws**-strum/ Any rigid extension of the anterior part of an *animal*.

S

SALIVARY GLAND /**sa**-li-veyr-ee …/ *Gland* that produces secretions for the *mouth*; in mollusks (MOLLUSCA) it secretes mucous onto the *radula*.

SALP /salp/ The common name for a tunicate in the class Thaliacea (CHORDATA-TUNICATA-**Thaliacea**).

SAND DOLLAR The common name for a highly flattened type of *irregular echinoid* (ECHINODERMATA-**Echinoidea**-**Irregularia**-Clypeasteroida).

SAPROZOIC /sap-ro-**zo**-ik/ Acquiring nutrition from dead organisms, or, as commonly used in reference to many *protists*, feeding via the absorption of dissolved organic and inorganic substances.

SARCOSTYLE /**sahr**-ko-stiyl/ See *nematophore*.

SCHIZOCOELY /**skiz**-zo-**see**-lee/ Type of *coelom* development whereby it forms from cavities that arise within the *mesoderm* (ANNELIDA, MOLLUSCA, ARTHROPODA, some DEUTEROSTOMIA). See also *enterocoely*.

SCHIZOGONY /ski-**zaw**-je-nee/ A mode of asexual reproduction in *protists* whereby the nucleus divides many times, and then the *cytoplasm* divides to make several new individuals. Synonymous with "merogony" and "multiple fission."

SCHIZONT /**skiz**-awnt/ Any stage in the life cycle of an apicomplexan in which the *parasite* is a multinucleate mass undergoing *schizogony*; the offspring are *merozoites* ([PROTISTA-CHROMALVEOLATA-STRAMENOPILES-APICOMPLEXA]).

SCLERITE /**skleyr**-riyt/ In general, any hardened structure, but most commonly used to identify parts of the arthropod *exoskeleton* (which consists of many discrete sections with flexible joints between them). See also *notum, pleuron, tergite, sternite,* and *sternum.*

SCLEROBLAST /**skleyr**-o-blast/ A *sponge* cell that makes *spicules* (PORIFERA). See also *calcioblast, founder cell, silicoblast* and *thickener cell.*

SCLEROSEPTA /skleyr-o-**sep**-tah/ **pl. scleroseptum** /skleyr-o-**sep**-tuhm/ The *calcareous* partitions secreted by the *epidermis* of the *pedal disc* in *coral polyps* (CNIDARIA-**Anthozoa** especially -**Hexacorallia**-Scleractinia).

SCLEROTIZE /**skleyr**-o-tiyz/ In general, to harden; used especially for the process in arthropods whereby the *exoskeleton* is hardened by the protein "sclerotin" (especially ARTHROPODA). See also *metecdysis.*

SCOLEX /**sko**-leks/ The organ in *tapeworms* bearing *suckers* and hooks, used in attaching to the *alimentary canal* wall of the host (PLATYHELMINTHES-**Cestoda**).

SCUTUM /**skyoo**-tuhm/ **pl. scuta** /**skyoo**-tah/ 1. The middle dorsal *thoracic* plate of insects (ARTHROPODA-HEXAPODA-**Insecta**). 2. In *barnacles,* in the plural, the two large plates that cover the anterior end of the body and, with the *terga,* form the *operculum* (ARTHROPODA-CRUSTACEA-**Maxillopoda**-**Cirripedia**).

SCYPHISTOMA /skiy-**fis**-to-mah/ In scyphozoans, the feeding *polyp* that forms from the *actinula* and becomes the *strobila*. It can *bud* off more scyphistomae asexually to make an aggregation of *polyps* (CNIDARIA-**Cubozoa**, -**Scyphozoa**).

SEA ANEMONES Common name for soft-bodied, solitary anthozoans (CNIDARIA-**Anthozoa**-**Hexacorallia**-Actiniaria, -Ceriantharia, -Corallimorpharia). See also *coral*.

SEA CUCUMBERS Common name for holothuroidean echinoderms (ECHINODERMATA-**Holothuroidea**).

SEA HARES Common name for a family of large, *shell*-less, marine gastropods (MOLLUSCA-**Gastropoda**-Aplysiidae).

SEA SPIDERS Common name for pycnogonids (ARTHROPODA-CHELICERATA-**Pycnogonida**).

SEA STARS Common name for asteroid echinoderms (ECHINODERMATA-**Asteroidea**). Synonymous with "starfish."

SEA URCHINS Common name for *regular echinoids* (ECHINODERMATA-**Echinoidea** except **Irregularia**).

SEGMENT Generally, one of many similar parts that join in succession to make a whole body, organ, or structure; segmentation can be superficial only, not extending all the way through the body or having any deep *embryologic* origin; the term "article" is usually used for a segment of an arthropod *appendage*. See also *annulus* (2), *metamere*, and *tagma*.

SEMINAL BURSA /**sem**-i-nahl **bur**-sah/ A *diverticulum* of the female genital *atrium* of *flatworms* in which *sperm* is deposited during copulation; the *sperm* later leave the seminal *bursa* to enter the *seminal receptacle*; in some cases it used to refer to the *seminal receptacle* of *flatworms* when no seminal *bursa* is present (PLATYHELMINTHES-**Trematoda**). See also *spermatheca*.

SEMINAL RECEPTACLE /**sem**-i-nahl .../ Any sac in which *sperm* are held until they can fertilize *ova*. See also *seminal bursa* and *spermatheca*.

SEMINAL VESICLE /**sem**-i-nahl .../ Any *gland* that adds nutrients or other secretions to the *sperm*.

SEPTAL FILAMENT /**sem**-i-nahl .../ See *mesenteric filament*.

SEPTUM /**sep**-tuhm/ Any membrane or thin plate that divides an organ or chamber, or that lies between two chambers, such as those inside the *shell* of a chambered nautilus (for example MOLLUSCA-**Cephalopoda**-<u>Nautilida</u>). See also *mesentery* and *sclerosepta*.

SESSILE /**se**-siyl/ Describing an organism that rests on or is affixed to a substrate and demonstrates limited locomotion.

SETA /**see**-tah/ **pl. setae** /**see**-tee/ Any bristle, especially like those found in annelids (especially ANNELIDA). Usually synonymous with "chaeta," although some distinguish the terms by microstructure or taxon.

SHELL The hardened outer covering of any organism; (often used as a more general term for any hard enclosure of an organism, even if internal, which should be called a *test*).

SHELL GLAND See *Mehlis' gland*.

SILICOBLAST /**si-li**-ko-blast/ Type of *spicule*-forming cell (*scleroblast*) in *sponges* that makes *spicules* out of silica (PORIFERA). See also *calcioblast*.

SILK A type of protein mixture (fibroin and related polypeptides) that emerges as a liquid and is hardened by the act of drawing it into a thread. See also *spinneret*.

SINISTRAL /**sin**-is-trahl/ Meaning "left-handed," it describes a gastropod shell that, when held with the apex (smallest whorls) up and the opening facing the observer, has its opening is to the left of the *columella* (MOLLUSCA-**Gastropoda**).

SINUS /**siy**-nuhs/ 1. Any cavity, recess, or passageway in an organ or body. See also *antrum*, *atrium*, *bursa*, *cecum*, *diverticulum*, and *lumen*. 2. The indentation of the *pallial line* in some burrowing bivalves (MOLLUSCA-**Bivalvia**).

SIPHON /**siy**-fuhn/ Any tube.

SIPHONOGLYPH /siy-**fah**-no-glif/ In anthozoans, a *ciliated, glandular* groove that extends down the length of one or both sides of the *actinopharynx* (absent or disputed in a few taxa); it is kept open even when the *mouth* is shut, helping to create high water pressure in the body column (CNIDARIA-**Anthozoa**).

SIPHONOZOOID /**siy**-fo-no-**zo**-id/ One of the modified *polyps* of a sea pansy colony (a type of soft *coral* within the order commonly called "sea pens") that pumps in water to keep the colony turgid (CNIDARIA-**Anthozoa**-**Octocorallia**-Pennatulacea-Renillidae).

SIPHUNCLE /si-**fuhn**-kuhl/ The cord of *visceral mass* that runs through the chambers of a cephalopod *shell*; it is used to release gas into the empty chambers for buoyancy (MOLLUSCA-**Cephalopoda**-Nautilida, -Sepiida, -Spirulida).

SKELETOZOID /**ske**-le-to-**zo**-id/ Type of *polyp* in the colonial hydrozoan *Hydractinia* that secretes a tough proteinaceous covering and thus keeps the other *polyps* from being crushed by objects that fall onto the colony (CNIDARIA-**Hydrozoa**-*Hydractinia*).

SLIME GLANDS The large *glands* in *velvet worms* that open on either side of the *mouth* and shoot out sticky secretions for defense and prey capture (ONYCHOPHORA).

SLUGS Casual term used for any oblong, soft animals without appendages, such as *sea cucumbers*, but more precisely used for *shell*-less gastropods (or those with highly reduced or internal *shells*), especially those on land (MOLLUSCA-**Gastropoda**).

SNAIL A common name that generally refers to any gastropod with a *shell*, most often used for those with coiled *shells* (i.e., not *limpets*) that lack a name already (such as whelks, conchs, and cowries), especialy terrestrial ones (MOLLUSCA-**Gastropoda**).

SOL /sol/ See *endoplasm* (1).

SOLENOCYTE /so-**len**-o-siyt/ A highly modified, complex *flame cell* in some annelids that has a *cilium* inside of a small tube.

SOMATOCOEL /so-**mat**-o-seel/ In echinoderm *embryos*, the most posterior of the three *coelomic* pouches formed by division of the original outpocketing of the *archenteron*. (ECHINODERMATA). See also *axocoel* and *hydrocoel*.

SOMITE /**so**-miyt/ In *embryology*, the beginnings of a *metamere*.

SORTING AREA The ridged and grooved anterior part of the molluscan *stomach* where smaller food particles are swept by *cilia* to the digestive *diverticula* and larger particles are swept to the *intestine* (MOLLUSCA).

SPERM The smaller, more mobile *gamete*. See also *gonad* and *testis*.

SPERM DUCT See *vas deferens*.

SPERMATHECA /spur-mah-**thee**-kah/ The *cuticle*-lined sac in female insects where *sperm* are stored and kept alive until needed (ARTHROPODA-HEXAPODA-**Insecta**). See also *seminal bursa* and *seminal receptacle*.

SPERMATOPHORE /spur-**mat**-o-for/ A structure containing *sperm*, given by males to females, especially in arachnids, insects, and cephalopods (especially ARTHROPODA-CHELICERATA-**Arachnida**, -HEXAPODA-**Insecta**, MOLLUSCA-**Cephalopoda**).

SPERMATOPHORIC GLAND /spur-**mat**-o-**for**-ic …/ *Gland* in male cephalopods that connects with the *vas deferens* and secretes the *spermatophore* (MOLLUSCA-**Cephalopoda**).

SPERMATOPHORIC SAC /spur-**mat**-to-**for**-ic …/ In cephalopods, the sac in males that stores his *spermatophores* before they are given to females (MOLLUSCA-**Cephalopoda**). Synonymous with "Needham's sac."

SPERMATOPOSITOR /spur-mat-to-**pah**-zi-tor/ A distinct, medial organ arachnid males use to give a *spermatophore* to females (ARTHROPODA-CHELICERATA-**Arachnida**).

SPERMIOCYST /**spur**-mee-o-sist/ In *sponges*, the encapsulated *sperm* inside the *carrier cell* (PORIFERA).

SPHERICAL SYMMETRY Body plan in which an organism can theoretically be divided into equal halves by cutting along any plane through its central point.

SPHINCTER /**sfink**-ter/ Any ring of muscle that controls the opening to a sac or tube.

SPICULE /**spik**-yool/ 1. In *sponges*, the *calcareous* or siliceous spines produced by *amoebocytes* and used in defense and support. They are important characters in *sponge taxonomy* (PORIFERA). 2. One of usually two *cuticular* rods used by male nematodes for opening the female *genital pore*; they are retractable and lie in pockets in the *cloaca* (NEMATODA).

SPINNERET /spi-ner-**et**/ Any *appendage* or organ that is modified for the release of *silk*. Spinnerets are famous in spiders (ARTHROPODA-CHELICERATA-**Arachnida**-Araneae) but are also found in symphylans (ARTHROPODA-MYRIAPODA-**Symphyla**) and various insects (especially the *larvae* of *holometabolous* ones) (ARTHROPODA-HEXAPODA-**Insecta**-**Pterygota** for example -Embiidina, -Lepidoptera).

SPINY-HEADED WORMS See *thorny-headed worms*.

SPIRACLE /**spi**-rah-kuhl/ A small, exterior opening for *tracheae* or *book lungs* in arthropods and onychophorans (ARTHROPODA, ONYCHOPHORA).

SPIRAL CLEAVAGE Type of *cleavage* in which the *blastomeres* on each level of the early *embryo* lie in between the *blastomeres* on the lower level; associated with *protostomes* and *determinate development*. Also called "spiralian cleavage." See also *Spiralia*, as well as *mesentoblast*, *teloblast*, and *radial cleavage*.

SPIRALIA /spiy-**ra**-lee-ah/ *Protostome* clade containing those phyla that usually demonstrate *spiral cleavage* ([ACANTHOCEPHALA], ANNELIDA, BRACHIOPODA, CYCLIOPHORA, ECTOPROCTA, ENTOPROCTA, GASTROTRICHA, GNATHOSTOMULIDA, MICROGNATHOZOA, MOLLUSCA, NEMERTEA, PHORONIDA, PLATYHELMINTHES, ROTIFERA).

SPIROCYST /**spiy**-ro-sist/ Type of *cnidocyst* characterized by having a thread armed with a complex adhesion mechanism but no barbs; in addition, in the undischarged state, the thread has both helical and lengthwise (accordion-like) pleats that significantly shorten its length (CNIDARIA). See also *nematocyst* and *ptychocyst.*

SPONGES Common name for poriferans (PORIFERA).

SPONGIN /**spuhn**-jin/ A tough, fibrous protein that is used for support in many *sponges* (PORIFERA).

SPONGOBLAST /**spuhn**-jo-blast/ Type of *sponge* cell that makes fibers out of *spongin* (PORIFERA).

SPONGOCOEL /**spuhn**-jo-seel/ In *asconoid* and *syconoid sponges*, the main cavity of the organism, which opens to the outside via the *osculum*; it is lined with *choanocytes* in *asconoid sponges* and is sometimes referred to as the "atrium" (PORIFERA).

SPOROCYST /**spor**-o-sist/ In *digenetic flukes*, the non-feeding *larval* stage that develops after the *miracidium* has entered the *intermediate host*; it gives rise to the *rediae* (PLATYHELMINTHES-**Trematoda**).

SPOROSAC /**spor**-o-sak/ A hydrozoan *medusa* that is more reduced than a *gonophore*, becoming nothing more than a gonad on the *polyp* (CNIDARIA-**Hydrozoa**).

SPOROZOITES /spor-o-**zo**-iyts/ In most apicomplexans, the life cycle stage that follows the *egg*. This stage enters the host and becomes a *schizont* (an asexually reproducing stage) ([PROTISTA-CHROMALVEOLATA-STRAMENOPILES-APICOMPLEXA]).

STALK 1. Any constriction that connects an organ, *appendage*, body section, or nest. 2. The preferred term in crinoids for the extension of the *aboral* surface that holds the organism above the substrate (ECHINODERMATA-**Crinoidea**). 3. The preferred term in entoprocts for the *segmented*, muscular extension that connects the *calyx* to the *attachment disc* (ENTOPROCTA). See also *pedicel, peduncle, petiole*, and *stolon*.

STARFISH See *sea star*.

STATOBLAST /**sta**-to-blast/ Produced asexually by freshwater ectoprocts, this is a small mass of *peritoneal* tissue that is *encysted* within a *chitinous* covering and is able to withstand difficult conditions; it becomes a new *zooid* when favorable conditions return (ECTOPROCTA).

STATOCYST /**sta**-to-sist/ A sensory structure that monitors the movement of an internal grain of calcium (the *statolith*) and thus can sense changes in position relative to the force of gravity.

STATOLITH /**sta**-to-lith/ A grain of calcium deposited in a *statocyst* which rolls against *cilia*, thus signaling the direction of the gravitational force.

STENOPODIUM /ste-no-**po**-dee-uhm/ Any thin, elongate crustacean *appendage* (ARTHROPODA-CRUSTACEA). Sometimes written as "stenopod."

STEREOBLASTULA /**ster**-ree-o-**gas**-troo-lah/ A *blastula* that lacks an internal cavity (i.e., lacks a *blastocoel*).

STEREOGASTRULA /**ster**-ree-o-**gas**-troo-lah/ A *gastrula* that lacks an *archenteron, blastopore*, or remnant *blastocoel*.

STERNITE /**stur**-niyt/ 1. A part of an arthropod *exoskeleton* (i.e., a *sclerite*) found on the ventral side, especially on the *abdomen* or *opisthosoma* (ARTHROPODA). 2. One of the two ventral plates on a kinorhynch *segment* (KINORHYNCHA).

STERNUM /**stur**-nuhm/ Any ventral, medial, outer, hardened structure; commonly used to refer to a medial *sternite* (especially ARTHROPODA).

STIGMA /**stig**-mah/ In euglenids, an aggregation of carotenoid pigments at the base of the reservoir that also gives rise to the long *flagellum*; it serves as a shield for the *photoreceptive* bodies at the base of the *flagellum* itself ([PROTISTA-EXCAVATA-EUGLENOZOA]). Sometimes also called an *eyespot*.

STOLON /**sto**-luhn/ Any *stalk*, root, or stem that runs along a substrate, generating and connecting multiple individuals. See also *pedicel, peduncle,* and *petiole*.

STOLONIFEROUS /**sto**-luhn-**i**-fur-uhs/ Type of colony formation in which the *zooids* are connected by a *stolon* (ECTOPROCTA). See also *arborescent* and *encrusting*.

STOMACH Any section of the *alimentary canal* that is somewhat enlarged and muscular, and that stores and churns food before moving it along.

STOMACH POUCH See *gastric pouch*.

STOMOBLASTULA /sto-mo-**blas**-chyoo-lah/ In *sponges*, the developmental stage characterized by a hollow ball of small and large cells, with inward-pointing *flagella* on the small cells and an opening in the middle of the large cells; it turns inside out to become either an *amphiblastula* or a *parenchymula* (PORIFERA).

STOMODEUM /sto-mah-**dee**-uhm/ The incipient anterior *alimentary canal* (*mouth, pharynx* [in part], *foregut*, and/or *actinopharynx*), formed by an external depression and inward migration of *ectodermal* tissue in the *embryo* or *larva*.

STONE CANAL In echinoderms, the section of the *water vascular system* that connects the *ring canal* to the *madreporite* (ECHINODERMATA).

STROBILA /**stro**-bi-luh/ In scyphozoans, the life cycle stage after the *scyphistoma*; it does not feed but instead pinches off several *ephyra* (*larval medusae*) from its *oral* end (CNIDARIA-**Cubozoa**, -**Scyphozoa**).

STYLET /**stiy**-let/ Any small, hard, piercing structure, such as in the mouthparts of *fleas* or at the end of a *ribbon worm proboscis*.

SUBCHELATE /**suhb**-**kee**-layt/ An arthropod claw formed by the terminal *article* being able to press back against the length of the penultimate *article*, such as in *praying mantids*, mantidflies (which are neuropteran insects), mantis shrimp, and amphipods (ARTHROPODA for example - HEXAPODA-**Insecta**-Mantodea, -Neuroptera-Mantispidae, ARTHROPODA-CRUSTACEA-**Malacostraca**-Stomatopoda, -**Malacostraca**-Amphipoda). See also *chela* and *gnathopods*.

SUBIMAGO /suhb-i-**may**-go / In *mayflies*, the developmental stage before the *imago* (*adult*) stage; unlike other insects, this stage in *mayflies* has wings, despite being sexually immature (ARTHROPODA-HEXAPODA-**Insecta**-Ephemeroptera).

SUBUMBRELLA /suhb-uhm-**brel**-lah/ The *oral* surface of a *medusa* (CNIDARIA).

SUBUMBRELLAR PIT One of four invaginations on the *subumbrellar* surface of scyphozoan *medusae*; also called a *"subumbrellar funnel"* (CNIDARIA-**Scyphozoa**).

SUCKER Any structure that is capable of producing a small vacuum and is thus able to stick to many surfaces, found in such places as at the ends of echinoderm *tube feet* (ECHINODERMATA) or on the *arms* of cephalopods (MOLLUSCA-**Cephalopoda**). See also *acetabulum* and *duo-gland system*.

SUGAR GLANDS Two *glands* in *chitons* that empty into the *esophagus*; they secrete enzymes that break polysaccharides down into simple sugars (MOLLUSCA-**Polyplacophora**).

SULCUS /**suhl**-kuhs/ In dinoflagellates, the longitudinal groove at right angles to the *annulus* that also contains a *flagellum* ([PROTISTA-CHROMALVEOLATA-ALVEOLATA-DINOZOA-DINOFLAGELLATA]). See also *annulus* (1).

SUPERFICIAL CLEAVAGE See *meroblastic cleavage*.

SYCONOID /**siy**-kuh-noyd/ Type of *sponge* body plan in which the body wall has many little *invaginations*, and water enters the *spongocoel* via *radial canals* (*flagellated chambers*) (PORIFERA-**Calcarea**). See also *asconoid* and *leuconoid*.

SYMBIOSIS /sim-biy-**yo**-sis/ Any close relationship between two species. See *mutualism*, *commensalism*, and *parasitism*.

SYMMETROGENIC FISSION /si-**met**-ro-**je**-nik …/ Type of longitudinal *binary fission* in *flagellated protists* that creates daughter cells that mirror each other (especially [PROTISTA-EXCAVATA-EUGLENOZOA-EUGLENIDA]). See also *homothetogenic fission*.

SYNCYTIUM /sin-**sish**-ee-uhm/ A combination of *cytoplasm* and several nuclei enclosed in a single membrane; sometimes further refined as originating from the *cytoplasmic* fusion of several cells, distinguishing it from a "coenocyte," which is used to describe multinucleate cells that result from divisions of the nucleus without full cell division.

SYNGAMY /**sin**-ga-mee/ The joining of *isogametes* in some *protists* ([PROTISTA]).

SYSTEMATICS /sis-te-**ma**-tiks/ The combination of *phylogenetics* and *taxonomy*; that is, the refinement of biological classification informed by advanced hypotheses of historical relationships.

SYZYGY /**si**-zi-jee/ The joining of two or more *gamonts* before the actual production of *gametes* or the joining of genetic material ([PROTISTA-CHROMALVEOLATA-STRAMENOPILES-APICOMPLEXA]).

T

TADPOLE LARVA Common name for the *larva* of tunicates (CHORDATA-TUNICATA).

TAGMA /tag-mah/ **pl. tagamata** /tag-**mah**-tah/ General term for a fundamental region of an arthropod body, such as the *prosoma* or *thorax*; tagmata likely result from the fusion of several *ancestral metameres* (ARTHROPODA).

TAPEWORMS Common name for cestodes (PLATYHELMINTHES-**Cestoda**).

TARSUS /**tahr**-suhs/ In general, the finely articulating parts of a *foot*, commonly used in arthropods to refer to the distal part (end) of a non-*chelate* leg or other *appendage* (like a *pedipalp*); a tarsus can consist of one to several *segments* (ARTHROPODA).

TAXONOMY /tak-**sah**-nah-mee/ The practice of assigning and revising scientific names and ranks in accordance with the biological naming system originally devised by Carl Linnaeus (1707–1778). See also *systematics*.

TECTIN /**tes**-tin/ A substance secreted by some shelled *protists* that has the toughness of the carbohydrate *chitin* but is a mixture of proteins and other carbohydrates ([PROTISTA-AMOEBOZOA-TUBULINEA-TESTACEALOBOSIA] for example *Difflugia*). Also called "pseudochitin."

TEGUMENT /**teg**-yoo-ment/ See *cuticle*.

TELOBLASTS /**tee**-lo-blasts/ Cells in early annelid *embryos* that result from divisions of the 4D cell and largely determine the segmented body plan of the adult (ANNELIDA). See also *mesentoblast*.

TELOLECITHAL /**tee**-lo-le-si-thal/ Type of *egg* that has its *yolk* on one side of the *cytoplasm*, such that the initial *meroblastic cleavage* of the *zygote* happens on one side of the *embryo*.

TELSON /**tel**-son/ A medial section at the very posterior of most arthropods; it bears the *anus* and has been speculated to be *homologous* to the annelid *pygidium*. It is not a *metamere*, and it bears no *appendages* (ARTHROPODA).

TENTACLE /**ten**-tah-kuhl/ **adj. tentacular** /ten-**tak**-yoo-lur/ Any long *appendage* used primarily in prey capture or tactile sensation.

TENTACULAR SHEATHS /ten-**tak**-yoo-lahr …/ In ctenophores, one of the two cavities in the sides of the body into which the *tentacles* can be withdrawn (CTENOPHORA).

TERGITE /**tur**-giyt/ 1. A part of an arthropod *exoskeleton* (i.e., a *sclerite*) found on the dorsal side, especially on the *abdomen* or *opisthosoma* (ARTHROPODA). 2. The dorsal plate on a kinorhynch *segment* (KINORHYNCHA).

TERGUM /**tur**-guhm/ **pl. terga** /**tur**-gah/ Generally referring to the dorsal side (like *notum*), used specifically in the plural for the two smaller plates that, with the *scuta*, form the *barnacle operculum* (ARTHROPODA-CRUSTACEA-**Maxillopoda-Cirripedia**).

TEST Any skeletal structure that surrounds most of the organism but is covered with tissue or *cytoplasm*.

TESTIS /**tes**-tis/ **pl. testes** /**tes**-teez/ An organ that produces *sperm* cells. See also *gamete* and *gonad*.

THICKENER CELL Type of *scleroblast* that works with the *founder cell* to produce a new *spicule* in *sponges*. It determines the thickness and size of the *spicule* (PORIFERA).

THORACIC LEGS /tho-**ra**-sik …/ The legs on an insect *larva* that ultimately develop into those on the *thorax* of the *adult*.

THORACOPOD /tho-**ra**-ko-pahd/ In crustaceans, any *appendage* attached to the *thorax*; these are further categorized into *maxillipeds* and *pereiopods* (ARTHROPODA-CRUSTACEA).

THORAX /**thor**-aks/ Generally, the section of the body between the head and the *abdomen*; used most commonly with hexapods (insects and allies), where it gives rise to the legs and, for most groups, wings (especially ARTHROPODA-HEXAPODA).

THORNY-HEADED WORMS Common name for members of the clade Acanthocephala, which are microscopic, *parasitic* worms that have a spine-covered *proboscis* they use to affix themselves to the *alimentary canals* of their hosts, which include invertebrates and vertebrates. They themselves lack an *alimentary canal*, and this, along with their *scolex*-like *proboscis*, make them and *tapeworms* a good study in convergent evolution. Recent *phylogenetic* studies suggest that acanthocephalans are actually members of the phylum Rotifera, and it has long been believed the two groups are closely related, at least. They are treated here simply as a group ([ACANTHOCEPHALA]). Synonymous with "spiny-headed worms."

TIEDEMANN'S BODIES Small, folded outpocketings of the echinoderm *ring canal* that may produce cells that circulate in the *water vascular system* (ECHINODERMATA).

TOE In Rotifers, one of two to four branches at the end of the *foot* through which the *adhesive gland* opens (ROTIFERA).

TORNARIA /tor-**nar**-ee-ah/ The *pelagic larva* of some hemichordates (HEMICHORDATA).

TORSION /**tor**-zhuhn/ In *slugs* and *snails*, the twisting of the body 180 degrees during the *veliger* stage so that the *mantle cavity* is over the head. The *alimentary canal* and nervous system are thus looped, and some paired organs are reduced to one (MOLLUSCA-**Gastropoda**).

TRACHEAE /**tray**-kee-ee/ **sing. trachea** /**tray**-kee-ah/ In onychophorans and many arthropods, the *cuticle*-lined tubes through which the organism receives air. They are highly branched, eventually leading to specific tissues and cells, and they open to the outside via *spiracles* (ARTHROPODA-CHELICERATA-**Arachnida**-Acari, -Opiliones, -Palpigradi, -Pseudoscorpionida, -Ricinulei, -Solifugae, ARTHROPODA-HEXAPODA-**Insecta**, ARTHROPODA-MYRIAPODA, ONYCHOPHORA). See also *tracheoles*.

TRACHEOLES /**tray**-kee-olz/ The finest branches of the *tracheal* system, which lead directly to the cells; they are made by special cells, and many can be made by only one cell (ARTHROPODA-CHELICERATA-**Arachnida**-Acari, Opiliones, -Palpigradi, -Pseudoscorpionida, -Ricinulei, -Solifugae, ARTHROPODA-HEXAPODA-**Insecta**, ARTHROPODA-MYRIAPODA, ONYCHOPHORA).

TREHALOSE /**tree**-hah-los/ A sugar common among arthropods and some other invertebrates, used especially as an energy source for flying insects and as a stabilizer which allows tardigrades and certain shrimp to survive desiccation (especially ARTHROPODA-CRUSTACEA-**Branchiopoda**, -HEXAPODA-**Insecta**, TARDIGRADA). See also *tun*.

TRICHOCYST /**tri**-ko-sist/ An *extrusome* found in many ciliates, it consists of a long thread that terminates in a barb ([PROTISTA-CHROMALVEOLATA-STRAMENOPILES-CILIOPHORA]). See also *cnidocyst*, *haptocyst*, and *nematocyst* (2).

TRILOBITE LARVA /**triy**-lo-biyt …/ The *larva* of *horseshoe crabs* (ARTHROPODA-CHELICERATA-**Merostomata**-Xiphosura).

TRIPLOBLASTIC /**trip**-lo-**blas**-tik/ Describing *embryos* with *ectoderm*, *endoderm*, and *mesoderm* (and describing any individual that develops from such an *embryo* or any taxon descended from such an ancestor); this state is not found in the *sponges* (PORIFERA) nor possibly the cnidarians and ctenophores (CNIDARIA, CTENOPHORA).

TRITOCEREBRUM /triy-to-**see-ree**-bruhm/ Section of the arthropod brain that receives information from and directs activity in the *mouth* (usually), the second *antennae* of crustaceans, and the *chelicerae* (ARTHROPODA). See also *deuterocerebrum* and *protocerebrum*.

TROCHOPHORE /**tro**-ko-for/ A type of *larva* that was originally defined as having two parallel bands of *cilia* around its circumference (the *metatroch* and the *prototroch*); these bands move water in opposite directions, bringing food to the *mouth*, which lies between them. The bands are also used for locomotion. However, this definition was later seen as too restrictive, with many *larvae* resembling

but not meeting it exactly; it is now defined as any *larva*
with a *prototroch* (especially ANNELIDA-**Echiura**,
-**Polychaeta**, ENTOPROCTA, MOLLUSCA,
SIPUNCULA).

TROCHUS /**tro**-kus/ An anterior ring of *cilia* on some
rotifer *coronas* that is positioned on a more anterior lobe
than is typical (ROTIFERA).

TROPHOZOITE /**tro**-fo-**zo**-iyt/ The feeding stage of
certain infectious *protists* with complex life cycles. In most
apicomplexans (such as those that cause *malaria*), the
term used to refer to a *merozoite* (the offspring of a
schizont) that has entered a red *blood* cell and is undergoing
enlargement, also known as the "ring stage"
([PROTISTA-CHROMALVEOLATA-
STRAMENOPILES-APICOMPLEXA]). It is also
commonly used to refer to the motile stage of the *parasite*
that causes *giardiasis* ([PROTISTA-EXCAVATA-
FORNICATA-EOPHARYNGIA-
DIPLOMONADIDA-GIARDIINAE]-*Giardia*).

TRUNK Vague term often used to refer to an elongate body
section that has few distinguishing features and yet
composes a significant portion of the organism; sometimes
interchanged with *abdomen*; sometimes referring to any
elongate *appendage*; used effectively in myriapods to refer to
their long, uniform, *leg*-bearing bodies posterior to the head
(ARTHROPODA-MYRIAPODA).

TUBE FOOT One of many external extensions of the *water
vascular system*, used in locomotion and food gathering. It
is filled with fluid and operated using hydraulic pressure
and thin muscles on its sides; many terminate in a *sucker*
(ECHINODERMATA). See also *duo-gland system*.

TUN /tuhn/ Tardigrade life stage during which metabolism is reduced to one ten-thousandths of the normal rate, almost all of the water is removed, and the cell membranes are chemically stabilized with *trehalose*; the *animal* can remain in this state of suspended animation for up to several years (TARDIGRADA).

TUNIC /**too**-nik/ The outer covering of tunicates. It can be colored or clear, tough or papery; it is mostly composed of protein and carbohydrates, but it can also have *amoeboid* cells and be supplied with *blood* vessels (CHORDATA-TUNICATA).

TYMPANUM /tim-**pa**-nuhm/ A sound-sensing structure in some insects in which tension receptors monitor changes in a membrane as it vibrates (ARTHROPODA-HEXAPODA-**Insecta**).

TYPHLOSOLE /**tiyf**-lo-sol/ Any infolding of the *alimentary canal*, especially in reference to the significant lobe that runs down the *intestine* of oligochaetes; it is an important structure for increasing the digestive surface area (especially ANNELIDA-**Oligochaeta**).

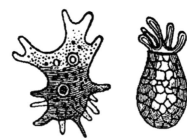

U, V, W

UMBO /**uhm**-bo/ The earliest part of a bivalve or brachiopod *shell*; in bivalves it is the most dorsal section of *shell*, and in brachiopods it is the most posterior (BRACHIOPODA, MOLLUSCA-**Bivalvia**).

UNDULATING MEMBRANE A structure in ciliates formed by the concentration and coordination of several *cilia* to make a long *fin*-like *organelle* used in feeding. The *cilia* are not fused, but their *basal bodies* are close enough for them to be highly coordinated ([PROTISTA-CHROMALVEOLATA-STRAMENOPILES-CILIOPHORA]). See also *ctene* and *membranelle*.

UNIRAMIA /**yoo**-ni-**ray**-mee-ah/ Obsolete *taxonomic* group that included the insects (ARTHROPODA-HEXAPODA-**Insecta**), myriapods (ARTHROPODA-MYRIAPODA), and, earlier, the *velvet worms* (ONYCHOPHORA), based on their *uniramous appendages*.

UNIRAMOUS /yoo-ni-**ray**-muhs/ Having only one branch, i.e., not forked, used mostly in reference to the *appendages* of arthropods (especially ARTHROPODA-CHELICERATA-**Arachnida**, -HEXAPODA-**Insecta**, -MYRIAPODA, ONYCHOPHORA). Recent studies in developmental biology and molecular *phylogenetics* suggest that *biramous* and uniramous *appendages* can be the result of different developmental processes and have evolved independently more than once in the arthropods. See also *Uniramia*.

UREA /yoo-**ree**-ah/ An organic compound (CO(NH$_2$)$_2$) used by some terrestrial invertebrates to remove *nitrogenous wastes*; it requires less water to eliminate than ammonia but more than *uric acid*.

URETER /yoo-**ree**-tur/ Any duct that connects a *kidney* to a *bladder*.

URETHRA /yoo-**ree**-thrah/ Any duct that leads from a *bladder* to the outside.

URIC ACID /**yur**-ik …/ A semisolid organic compound (C$_5$H$_4$N$_4$O$_3$) used to remove *nitrogenous waste* by insects and other *animals* that need to conserve water.

UROCHORDATA /**yur**-o-kor-**dah**-tah/ Former (and still commonly used) name for the chordate subphylum Tunicata.

UROPODS /**yoor**-o-pahdz/ The most posterior pair of *abdominal appendages* in crustaceans; when present, they are often specialized for swimming, jumping, respiration, or reproduction (ARTHROPODA-CRUSTACEA). See also *pleopod*.

UTERUS /**yoo**-ter-uhs/ **adj. uterine** /**yoo**-ter-een/ Any organ that holds fertilized *eggs* that are ready to be released, such as in *tapeworms* (for example PLATYHELMINTHES-**Cestoda**).

VAGINA Any structure specialized for the reception of *sperm*.

VALVE One part of a multi-part *shell*, such as that of a *clam* (for example MOLLUSCA-**Bivalvia**).

VAS DEFERENS /vas **de**-fer-enz/ Any tube that carries *sperm* from the *vas efferens* or *testes* to the *seminal vesicle*. Synonymous with "sperm duct."

VAS EFFERENS /vas **ef**-fer-enz/ Any tube that carries *sperm* from the *testes* to the *vas deferens*.

VEGETAL POLE The hemisphere of the *blastula* that is comprised of large, *yolky* cells (*macromeres*), which divide more slowly than those of the *animal pole*.

VELARIUM /ve-**ler**-ee-uhm/ In the *medusae* of *box jellyfish*, a structure that resembles a hydrozoan *velum* (a flange around the *bell*) but which has a different *embryonic* origin (CNIDARIA-**Cubozoa**).

VELIGER /**vee**-li-juhr/ A shelled *larval* form in mollusks that develops from the *trochophore*. It has *cilia*, a *foot*, and a *mantle cavity* (MOLLUSCA [except for **Polyplacophora**]).

VELUM /**vee**-luhm/ A shelf of tissue around the *bell* of hydrozoan *medusa*; it creates a lip or restricted opening to the cavity created by the concave *subumbrella* (CNIDARIA-**Hydrozoa**). See also *velarium*.

VELVET WORMS Common name for onychophorans (ONYCHOPHORA).

VENTRAL SINUS In crustaceans, the area in the ventral *thorax* that collects *blood* from all parts of the body before it passes to the *gills* and then to the *heart* (ARTHROPODA-CRUSTACEA).

VENTRICLE /**ven**-tri-kuhl/ 1. Any cavity within an organ. 2. The chamber in a *heart* where *blood* is held before being pumped away from the *heart*.

VERMIFORM /**vur**-mi-form/ Worm-like in overall morphology (elongate and with no, few, or reduced *appendages*).

VERMIFORM LARVA /**vur**-mi-form …/ The asexually produced *larva* of dicyemids (DICYEMIDA).

VERRILL'S ORGAN /**ver**-rilz …/ See *funnel organ.*

VERTEBRAE /**ver**-te-bray/ **sing. vertebra** /**ver**-te-brah/
In ophiuroids, the articulated *ossicles* that join together
along the length of the *arms.* They occupy most of the
interior of each *arm* and have sockets by which they
connect to each other (ECHINODERMATA-
Ophiuroidea).

VESTIGIAL /ves-**ti**-jee-ahl/ Describing an incompletely or
ineffectively developed structure or organ that may be
the remnant of what was once a useful organ in an
ancestor.

VIBRACULUM /viy-**brak**-yoo-luhm/ A specialized
ectoproct *heterozooid* in which the *operculum* is modified
into a long bristle that sweeps back and forth, removing
debris (ECTOPROCTA-**Gymnolaemata**). See also
avicularium.

VISCERAL MASS /**vi**-ser-ahl …/ In mollusks, the somewhat
vague body section that is dorsal to the *foot,* covered by the
mantle, and houses the organs (MOLLUSCA).

VITELLARIA /vi-tel-**leyr**-ee-uh/ 1. In crinoids and some
sea cucumbers, a non-feeding *larva* that is cylindrical and has
transverse *ciliated* bands (essentially, a non-feeding
doliolaria); continued *metamorphosis* leads to the *pentactula*
(ECHINODERMATA-**Crinoidea**, -**Holothuroidea**).
2. The specialized organs in *flatworms* that make *yolk* and
contribute to the *egg* shell; vitellaria are separate from the
ovaries and connect with them at the *ootype*; sometimes
"vitellaria" is used to refer only to the junction of two
"vitelline ducts" (the *yolk*-producing extensions of this
system) (PLATYHELMINTHES). Synonymous with
"vitelline glands" and "yolk glands."

VITELLINE GLANDS /vi-tel-**leen** …/ See *vitellaria* (2).

VIVIPARY /viy-**vip**-uh-ree/ Mode of reproduction in which the *embryo* develops within the mother and is nourished by her until capable of living, to some degree, independently. See also *ovipary* and *ovovivipary*.

WATER BEARS Common name for tardigrades (TARDIGRADA).

WATER-VASCULAR SYSTEM In echinoderms, the network of tubes inside the *coelom* that is connected to the outside (to the *coelomic* fluids in *sea cucumbers*) via the *madreporite*, and that maintains the fluid pressure needed to operate the *tube feet*. The interior of the system is *ciliated*, and the fluid, although much like sea water, does contain free-living cells, some protein, and extra potassium (ECHINODERMATA).

WHEEL ORGAN 1. A series of *ciliated* ridges or projections inside the *buccal cavity* of cephalochordates, lying directly before the opening to the *pharynx* (CHORDATA-CEPHALOCHORDATA).
2. Alternative name for the rotifer *corona* (ROTIFERA).

WING PADS The tissues in insect *larvae* that give rise to functional wings at the final *molt* (or, in *mayflies*, the penultimate *molt*); they are often visible externally in *hemimetabolous* orders.

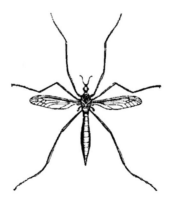

X, Y, Z

XENOTURBELLIDS /**zee**-no-tuhr-**bel**-lidz/
Anatomically simple marine worms in the genus
Xenoturbella, which appear to be closely related to the
acoelomorphs; there is molecular evidence that the
xenoturbellids and *acoelomorphs* together constitute a
distinct phylum, Xenacoelomorpha, which is sister either
to the *Nephrozoa* or to just the *protostomes*.

X-ORGAN A *neurosecretory* structure (i.e., a *gland*) in the
eyestalks of some crustaceans that produces hormones
important in reproduction, *molting*, and metabolism
(ARTHROPODA-CRUSTACEA). See also *y-organ*.

XYLOPHAGOUS /ziy-lo-**fay**-guhs/ Describing an
organism that eats wood, such as termites (for example
ARTHROPODA-HEXAPODA-**Insecta-Pterygota-**
Isoptera).

YOLK A nutritive substance (mostly proteins and lipids)
secreted with *eggs* that aids in the development of the
embryo. Also called "vitelline."

YOLK GLANDS See *vitellaria*.

YOLK PYRAMIDS The conical divisions of *yolk* in a
centrolecithal embryo that extend from the outer layer of
cytoplasm to the *yolk* center.

YOLK SAC A membrane that holds together an *embryo* and
its *yolk*.

Y-ORGAN A type of endocrine tissue (i.e., a *gland*) in crustaceans that releases *ecdysone*, a hormone important in *molting* (ARTHROPODA-CRUSTACEA). See also *x-organ*.

ZOEA /zo-ee-ah/ **pl. zoeae** /zo-ee-ee/ **or zoeas** /zo-ee-ahz/ In decapods, this is the *larval* stage that follows the *nauplius larva* (sometimes with "pseudometanauplius," "metanauplius," and/or "protozoea" stages in between); it has a long *rostrum* and head spine; in certain crabs it is followed by a *megalops larva* (ARTHROPODA-CRUSTACEA-**Malacostraca**-Decapoda).

ZOOCHLORELLAE /zo-klo-**rel**-lee/ Photosynthetic *protists* mostly in the genus *Chlorella* ([PROTISTA-ARCHAEPLASTIDA, which also includes plants]) that are *symbiotic* with certain invertebrate *animals* and ciliates (CNIDARIA, PLATYHELMINTHES, [PROTISTA-CHROMALVEOLATA-STRAMENOPILES-CILIOPHORA]).

ZOOID /**zo**-id/ A single individual within a colony (for example CHORDATA-TUNICATA-**Ascidiacea**, CNIDARIA, especially ECTOPROCTA).

ZOOXANTHELLAE /zo-zan-**thel**-lee/ Dinoflagellates ([PROTISTA-CHROMALVEOLATA-DINOFLAGELLATA]) that are commonly found in the cells of various invertebrates (most famously *corals*) and even the *cytoplasm* of some other *protists* (ciliates), where they photosynthesize for their and their host's benefit (for example CNIDARIA-**Anthozoa-Hexacorallia**-Scleractinia, MOLLUSCA-**Bivalvia**-Cardiidae-Tridacninae, PORIFERA, [PROTISTA-CHROMALVEOLATA- CILIOPHORA], [XENACOELOMORPHA-ACOELOMORPHA]).

ZYGOTE /**ziy**-got/ The unicellular stage of development immediately after the union of *gametes*.

Synonyms

abdomen, Chelicerata = opisthoma = opisthosoma

aboral, Cnidaria medusa = exumbrella

Acanthocephala = thorny-headed worms = spiny-headed worms

acorn worms = Hemichordata

actinopodium = axopodium

adult, Insecta = imago

alimentary canal = gut

alimentary canal, Cnidaria and Ctenophora = gastrovascular cavity

amphioxi = lancelets = Cephalochordata

antennal gland = green gland

Anthozoa = sea anemones

antrum = atrium = bursa = cecum = diverticulum = lumen = sinus

Aplysiidae = sea hares

arrow worms = Chaetognatha

ascus = compensation sac

Asteroidea = starfish = sea stars

atrial siphon/canal = exhalant siphon/canal, Tunicata = excurrent siphon/canal, Tunicata

atrium = bursa = cecum = diverticulum = lumen = sinus = antrum

axial gland = axial organ

axial organ = axial gland

axopodium = actinopodium

barnacles = Cirripedia

basal body = kinetosome

basket stars = Ophiuroidea, with branched arms

beetles = Coleoptera

bladder worm = cysticercus

box jellyfish = Cubozoa

brachial valve = dorsal valve

brittle stars = Ophiuroidea, except basket stars

buccal = oral

buccal siphon/canal = inhalant siphon/canal, Tunicata = incurrent siphon/canal, Tunicata = oral siphon/canal

bugs = Heteroptera

bursa = cecum = diverticulum = lumen = sinus = antrum = atrium

calymma = extracapsular cytoplasm = extracapsulum

cecum = diverticulum = lumen = sinus = antrum = atrium = bursa

cell membrane = plasmalemma

Cephalochordata = amphioxi = lancelets

Cestoda = tapeworms

chaeta = seta

Chaetognatha = arrow worms

choanocyte = collar cell

choanocyte chamber = flagellated chamber = radial canal, syconoid sponges

ciliated loop = corona, Chaetognatha = corona ciliata

Cirripedia = barnacles

Clypeasteroida = sand dollars

cnida = cnidocyst

cnidoblast = cnidocyte = nematocyst, Cnidaria

cnidocyst = cnida

cnidocyte = nematocyst, Cnidaria = cnidoblast

Coleoptera = beetles

collar = mesosome, Hemichordata

collar cell = choanocyte

comb = ctene

compensation sac = ascus

complete metamorphosis = indirect development = holometabolism

corona ciliata = ciliated loop = corona, Chaetognatha

corona, Chaetognatha = corona ciliata = ciliated loop

corona, Rotifera = wheel organ, Rotifera

ctene = comb

Cubozoa = box jellyfish

cuticle = tegument

cysticercus = bladder worm

daddy longlegs = Opiliones = harvestmen

digestive cecum, Asteroidea = digestive gland, Asteroidea = hepatic cecum, Asteroidea = pyloric cecum, Asteroidea

digestive gland, Asteroidea = hepatic cecum, Asteroidea = pyloric cecum, Asteroidea = digestive cecum, Asteroidea

digestive gland, Mollusca = liver, Mollusca

direct development = hemimetabolism = incomplete metamorphosis

diverticulum = lumen = sinus = antrum = atrium = bursa = cecum

dorsal valve = brachial valve

Echinoidea, regular = sea urchins

ectoplasm = gel

egg = ovum = macrogamete

endoplasm, Radiolaria = intracapsular cytoplasm

endoplasm = sol

Ephemeroptera = mayflies

epidermis, Arthropoda = hypodermis

excurrent siphon/canal, Tunicata = atrial siphon/canal = exhalant siphon/canal, Tunicata

exhalant siphon/canal, Tunicata = atrial siphon/canal = excurrent siphon/canal, Tunicata

extracapsular cytoplasm = extracapsulum = calymma

extracapsulum = calymma = extracapsular cytoplasm

exumbrella = aboral, Cnidaria medusa

eyespot = ocellus (simplest)

eyespot, Protista = stigma

fangs, Chilopoda = forcipule = poison claws

feces, Insecta = frass

flagellated chamber = radial canal, syconoid sponges = choanocyte chamber

flukes = Trematoda

forcipule = poison claws = fangs, Chilopoda

frass = feces, Insecta

funnel organ = organ of Verrill

gastric filament = septal filament = mesenteric filament

gastric pouch = stomach pouch

Gastropoda, with shallow, conical shell = limpets

gastrovascular cavity = alimentary canal, Cnidaria and Ctenophora gel = ectoplasm

gill slits = pharyngeal slits, Hemichordata

gladius = pen

Gnathostomulida = jaw worms

Gordian worms = hairworms = horsehair worms = Nematomorpha

green gland = antennal gland

gut = alimentary canal

hairworms = horsehair worms = Nematomorpha = Gordian worms

harvestmen = daddy longlegs = Opiliones

heart urchins = Spatangoida

Hemichordata = acorn worms

hemimetabolism = incomplete metamorphosis = direct development

hepatic cecum, Asteroidea = pyloric cecum, Asteroidea = digestive cecum, Asteroidea = digestive gland, Asteroidea

hermaphroditic = monoecious

Heteroptera = bugs

Hirudinea = leeches

holometabolism = complete metamorphosis = indirect development

Holothuroidea = sea cucumbers

horsehair worms = Nematomorpha = Gordian worms = hairworms

horseshoe crabs = Xiphosura

hypodermis = epidermis, Arthropoda

imago = adult, Insecta

incomplete metamorphosis = hemimetabolism = direct development

incurrent siphon/canal, Tunicata = buccal siphon/canal = inhalant siphon/canal, Tunicata = oral siphon/canal

indirect development = holometabolism = complete metamorphosis

inhalant siphon/canal, Tunicata = buccal siphon/canal = incurrent siphon/canal, Tunicata = oral siphon/canal

intracapsular cytoplasm = endoplasm, Radiolaria

jaw worms = Gnathostomulida

jellyfish = medusa

kidney = nephridium

kinetosome = basal body

lancelets = Cephalochordata = amphioxi

leeches = Hirudinea

limpets = Gastropoda, with shallow, conical shell

liver, Mollusca = digestive gland, Mollusca

Lophotrochozoa = Spiralia

lumen = sinus = antrum = atrium = bursa = cecum = diverticulum

macrogamete = egg = ovum

Mantodea = praying mantids/mantises

mayflies = Ephemeroptera

medusa = jellyfish

megalops = postlarva

Mehlis' gland = shell gland

meroblastic cleavage = superficial cleavage

merogony = multiple fission = schizogony

mesenteric filament = gastric filament = septal filament

mesosome, Hemichordata = collar

metasoma = postabdomen

microgamete = sperm

monoecious = hermaphroditic

mother-of-pearl = nacre

multiple fission = schizogony = merogony

myxopodium = reticulopodium = rhizopodium

nacre = mother-of-pearl

Needham's sac = spermatophoric sac

nematocyst, Cnidaria = cnidoblast = cnidocyte

Nematomorpha = Gordian worms = hairworms = horsehair worms

nematophore = sarcostyle

Nemertea = ribbon worms = Rhynchocoela

nephridium = kidney

nerve net = plexus

ocellus (simplest) = eyespot

Onychophora = velvet worms

ooecium = ovicell

Ophiuroidea, except basket stars = brittle stars

Ophiuroidea, with branched arms = basket stars

Opiliones = harvestmen = daddy longlegs

opisthoma = opisthosoma = abdomen, Chelicerata

opisthosoma = abdomen, Chelicerata = opisthoma

oral = buccal

oral siphon/canal = buccal siphon/canal = inhalant siphon/canal, Tunicata = incurrent siphon/canal, Tunicata

organ of Verrill = funnel organ

organ-pipe coral = *Tubipora*

ovicell = ooecium

ovivipary = ovovivipary = ovoviviparity

ovoviviparity = ovivipary = ovovivipary

ovovivipary = ovoviviparity = ovivipary

ovum = macrogamete = egg

Oxyuridae = pinworms

pallial groove = pallial line

pallial line = pallial groove

pedicel = peduncle = petiole = stalk

peduncle = petiole = stalk = pedicel

pen = gladius

petiole = stalk = pedicel = peduncle

pharyngeal slits, Hemichordata = gill slits

phasmid = stick insect

Physalia = Portuguese man-of-war

pinworms = Oxyuridae

plasmalemma = cell membrane

plexus = nerve net

podium = tube foot

poison claws = fangs, Chilopoda = forcipule

Porifera = sponges

Portuguese man-of-war = *Physalia*

postabdomen = metasoma

postlarva = megalops

praying mantids/mantises = Mantodea

pseudochitin = tectin

Pycnogonida = sea spiders

pyloric cecum, Asteroidea = digestive cecum, Asteroidea = digestive gland, Asteroidea = hepatic cecum, Asteroidea

radial canal, syconoid sponges = choanocyte chamber = flagellated chamber

reticulopodium = rhizopodium = myxopodium

rhizopodium = myxopodium = reticulopodium

Rhynchocoela = Nemertea = ribbon worms

ribbon worms = Rhynchocoela = Nemertea

salps = Thaliacea

sand dollars = Clypeasteroida

sarcostyle = nematophore

schizogony = merogony = multiple fission

sea anemones = Anthozoa

sea cucumbers = Holothuroidea

sea hares = Aplysiidae

sea spiders = Pycnogonida

sea stars = Asteroidea = starfish

sea urchins = Echinoidea, regular

septal filament = mesenteric filament = gastric filament

seta = chaeta

shell gland = Mehlis' gland

sinus = antrum = atrium = bursa = cecum = diverticulum = lumen

sol = endoplasm

Spatangoida = heart urchins

sperm = microgamete

sperm duct = vas deferens

spermatophoric sac = Needham's sac

spiny-headed worms = Acanthocephala = thorny-headed worms

Spiralia = Lophotrochozoa

sponges = Porifera

stalk = pedicel = peduncle = petiole

starfish = sea stars = Asteroidea

stick insect = phasmid

stigma = eyespot, Protista

stomach pouch = gastric pouch

superficial cleavage = meroblastic cleavage

tadpole larva = Tunicata larva

tapeworms = Cestoda

Tardigrada = water bears

tectin = pseudochitin

tegument = cuticle

Thaliacea = salps

thorny-headed worms = spiny-headed worms = Acanthocephala

Trematoda = flukes

tube foot = podium

Tubipora = organ-pipe coral

Tunicata larva = tadpole larva

vas deferens = sperm duct

velvet worms = Onychophora

vitellaria = vitelline glands = yolk glands

vitelline glands = yolk glands = vitellaria

water bears = Tardigrada

wheel organ, Rotifera = corona, Rotifera

Xiphosura = horseshoe crabs

yolk glands = vitellaria = vitelline glands

Readings

Adl, S.M., Simpson, A.G., Farmer, M.A., Andersen, R.A., Anderson, O.R., Barta, J.R., Bowser, S.S., Brugerolle, G.U.Y., Fensome, R.A., Fredericq, S. and James, T.Y. 2005. The new higher level classification of eukaryotes with emphasis on the taxonomy of protists. *Journal of Eukaryotic Microbiology*, 52(5): 399-451.

Barnes, R.D. 1987. *Invertebrate Zoology*, Fifth Edition. Fort Worth: Saunders College Publishing/Harcourt Brace.

Beklemishev, W.N. 1969. *Principles of Comparative Anatomy of Invertebrates. I. Promorphology.* Chicago: University of Chicago Press. [Translated by J.M. McLennan.]

Boxshall, G.A. and Jaume, D. 2009. Exopodites, epipodites and gills in crustaceans. *Arthropod Systematics and Phylogeny*, 67(2): 229–254.

Brusca, R.C. and Brusca, G.J. 2003. *Invertebrates*, Second Edition. Sunderland, MA: Sinauer Associates.

Conn, D.B. and Swiderski, Z. 2008. A standardised terminology of the embryonic envelopes and associated developmental stages of tapeworms (Platyhelminthes: Cestoda). *Folia Parasitologica*, 55(1): 42–52.

Daly, M., Brugler, M.R., Cartwright, P., Collins, A.G., Dawson, M.N., Fautin, D.G., France, S.C., McFadden, C.S., Opresko, D.M., Rodriguez, E. and Romano, S.L. 2007. The phylum Cnidaria: a review of phylogenetic patterns and diversity 300 years after Linnaeus. *Zootaxa*, 1668: 127–182.

Edgecombe, G.D., Giribet, G., Dunn, C.W., Hejnol, A., Kristensen, R.M., Neves, R.C., Rouse, G.W., Worsaae,

K., and Sørensen, M.V. 2011. Higher-level metazoan relationships: recent progress and remaining questions. *Organisms Diversity & Evolution*, 11(2): 151–172.

Henry, J.Q. 2014 Spiralian model systems. *International Journal of Developmental Biology*, 58: 389–401.

Hickman, C.P., Roberts, L.S., and Hickman, F.M. 1990. *Biology of Animals*, Fifth Edition. St. Louis: Times Mirror/Mosby Publishing.

Hyman, L. 1940. *The Invertebrates. Vol. 1, Protozoa through Ctenophora*. New York: McGraw-Hill.

— 1951. *The Invertebrates. Vol. 2, Platyhelminthes and Rhynchocoela*. New York: McGraw-Hill.

— 1951. *The Invertebrates. Vol. 3, Acanthocephala, Aschelminthes, and Entoprocta*. New York: McGraw-Hill.

— 1955. *The Invertebrates. Vol. 4, Echinodermata*. New York: McGraw-Hill.

— 1959. *The Invertebrates. Vol. 5, Smaller Coelomate Groups*. New York: McGraw-Hill.

— 1967. *The Invertebrates. Vol. 6, Mollusca I, Aplacophora, Polyplacophora, Monoplacophora, Gastropoda: The Coelomate Bilateria*. New York: McGraw-Hill.

Kayal, E., Roure, B., Philippe, H., Collins, A.G. and Lavrov, D.V. 2013. Cnidarian phylogenetic relationships as revealed by mitogenomics. *BMC Evolutionary Biology*, 13(1): 1–18.

Kozloff, E.N. 1990. *Invertebrates*. New York: Saunders College Publishing/Harcourt Brace.

Rouse, G.W., Wilson, N.G., Carvajal, J.I. and Vrijenhoek, R.C. 2016. New deep-sea species of *Xenoturbella* and the position of Xenacoelomorpha. *Nature*, 530(7588): 94–97.

van Cleave, H.J. 1932. Eutely or Cell Constancy in Its Relation to Body Size. *The Quarterly Review of Biology*, 7(1): 59-67.

Illustrations

From *A Manual of Zoology*, Second Edition, 1871, by Henry
Alleyne Nicholson:

CPSIA information can be obtained
at www.ICGtesting.com
Printed in the USA
FSOW02n1935030516
20029FS

9 781530 670024